The Wonders of a Walk in the Woods

One Man's Inspired Journey to Protect and Enjoy the Woods and Wildlife

by

John Rockenbaugh

The Wonders of a Walk in the Woods
One Man's Inspired Journey to Protect and Enjoy the Woods and Wildlife
By John Rockenbaugh

ISBN 978-1516884926

"Nature will bear the closest inspection.
She invites us to lay our eye level with her smallest leaf,
and take an insect view of its plain."
Thoreau

In affection and gratitude,
"The Wonders of a Walk in the Woods"
is dedicated in memory of
a wonderful educator and lover of nature,
my loving husband and best friend of 40 years,
John Rockenbaugh,

And to our children, Brodie, Caleb, Timothy (TJ) and Tracie,
and our grandchildren, Elijah, Carter, Quinn,
Conor, Owen, Brooks, Griffin and Nolan,
who are the love of our lives.

"I came to the woods because I wished to live deliberately,
to front only the essential facts of life,
and see if I could not learn what it had to teach
and not when I came to die,
discover that I had not lived."
Thoreau

In the Beginning

My earliest recollection of not playing-it-safe was in the friendly company of Nature.

As a second grader, my newest collection of matchbook covers featured the colorful American songbirds of 1959 in their natural settings. I took the pasted-to-cardboard set to the West School to share with classmates. My snappish white-haired teacher didn't approve of my enthusiasm and said that I was wrong to disrupt class by bringing them. I was to forget about the birds, sit down, and remain quiet for 24 years!

Her lesson, though never understood, would never be forgotten!

The following year, across the hall, I contributed 4 mammal life history stories to the third grade's "The First Book of Animals." They included: "The Otter," "The Porcupine," "The Raccoon," and "The Skunk." A check mark on my grade card indicated that I was aware of the world around me. I knew it was a belated checkmark.

During the formative years, Nature continued to influence my life. Day hikes to the riparian habitats of nearby Mill Creek led to discoveries of blue herons, clear ripples, stinging nettles, and ethereal peacefulness.

In 1962, my parents purchased all the wilderness I needed in a worn-out farm just west of Marysville, Ohio.

Our home remained in town where tree lawns were planted with maples, elms, and coniferous utility poles. The graceful limbs of our neighbors towering elm provided welcome summer shade and a site for the woven hanging nests that gently cradled countless generations of Baltimore orioles.

Youthful 4-H projects always included Nature and the farm. They allowed me to live life on my terms until 1968. A fiery tongue-lashing by a dominating 4-H advisor, over philosophical differences in Junior Leadership responsibilities, ended my association with 4-H at the completion of that year.

It was another lesson neither understood, nor forgotten.

I drew upon the presence of profound principles that had been sown in my soul. The germinating convictions would emerge to serve Nature, and then ripen to defend it from the stacked-deck of blind progress in America.

In July of 1973, as man and wife, planning began on my truly God-inspired "The Woods Nature Reserve." Twenty eight acres of third growth oak and hickory would be preserved within my parents' humble farm. The farm contained many secrets. In due time, each would be revealed.

Ten years later, The Ohio Department of Transportation (ODOT), said that it would be futile—and a big mistake—to question their detailed plans to destroy our family's dreams. After all, a new limited access 4-lane highway, diagonally—perfect through our Nature reserve—would encourage and allow much more progress to come to Union County.

It was disappointing to learn that my textbook understanding of how our government and its agencies operated was a cruel myth. All of my school teachers had failed to reveal how a representative republic, albeit a capitalistic regime, really works.

Autocratic highway elders told me to forget the birds, sit down, and be quiet—for they had a highway to build! Their well-rehearsed admonishments sounded hauntingly familiar.

It was time to stand up for the things of Nature by confronting the established untouchables of "Progress in America." I shoved back hard in all directions with both arms fully extended upon my wife's '60's model manual typewriter.

Inexplicably, Nature had prepared me to recognize, challenge, and overcome the threats facing our vanishing natural world. Playing it safe was not an option.

The Rockenbaugh Farm, 1962

On February 25, 1804, President Thomas Jefferson granted this portion of the Northwest Territory to two soldiers and two sergeants. Without seeing it, they sold it to an opportunistic lawyer… and so on and so forth!

The Shawnee Nation knew it as a contiguous land without boundaries, restrictions, or designations. These men never knew it.

On November 13, 1962, the Davis farm became the Rockenbaugh farm: one-hundred acres belonging to the 800 acre tract of Virginia Military Survey #1913.

This latest transaction was entered and duly recorded three miles east at the Union County Courthouse. Contrary to its designation, the highest and best use of the farm was not production agriculture, but Nature.

Although under qualified to grow proper crops, it was eager to grow oak and hickory.

The farm's frontage was along a modernized two-lane US Rt. 33, two miles west of Marysville, Ohio. Locals referred to the highway as the Bellefontaine Road—the next town of any size west. Earlier generations knew it as the Columbus & Bellefontaine Gravel Road, then a day trip of 60 miles to, or from, our capital city.

It seemed like any other farm of its era, a simple 1 1/2 story frame house, 3 barns, a cement slab silo, 4 fields, and distant green woods all along the south-to southeast horizon. A seasonally wet ditch began at the barns' old downspouts and hustled across the farm into the Gulf of Mexico. Simply stated, It was 12.5 acres long (north to south) by 8 acres wide.

A large billboard was inherited, as well as two smaller roadside signs that proclaimed the virtues of an antique store and the benefits of an insect pest control business in town: two professions that continued to prosper and grow; one as the result of, and the other in spite of, so-called progress.

The fenced-in barnyard featured discarded railroad ties as posts. Train, after train, had failed to crush the scent of creosote that lingered on warm afternoons. Behind the shake shingle-roofed wooden barn, a water trough was fabricated from a tall cast-iron boiler. It was laid upon its side, cut in half lengthwise, and welded together. A one inch diameter steel pipe, wired overhead to the joists, transported water across the barn to fill the trough in eight hours' time. I used to marvel at its cool, clear, and continuous stream. I wondered where the clean cold water came from and how the lifting of a handle made it flow.

In an adjacent lot grew a tall cottonwood and a scattering of catalpa trees. These were familiar landmarks to the hardened cottontails that darted among irregularly spaced piles of hoarded used boards and mounds of scrap metal skeletons. A rusty-red buzz saw sat lopsided amidst graying tree stumps and tall fescue.

Without fear of contradiction, one could read the indelible entries of the farm's faded diary that preceded our ownership. It was yet another work of non-fiction from the generation that lived, survived, and never forgot the material losses of The Great Depression.

Dividing the farm nearly in half is an old earthen roadbed that runs north to south without issue. There are two fields on the east and two fields on the west. The road divides the woods as well. It follows the gentle terrain and measures 25' across from the centerlines of the hand-dug ditches on either side. The 2365 foot long road through our property was surveyed in April of 1853 and was known as the Turner Road Extension. It linked Turner Road and the old Columbus & Bellefontaine Gravel Road with State Route 245.

The Paris Township road, designed for horses and wagons, remained opened until June of 1950. By then, the farm's former owner was tiring of timid midnight knocks upon his locked front door.

Red-faced lovers would beg the assistance of his sound asleep tractor to pull out their mired-in-the-mud Ford. This unmapped, but well-known lover's lane was petitioned for abandonment that year and closed in 1951. It became a legal part of the farm and ended an era of two and four door romance.

At the time of purchase by our family, the road was neatly blocked at either end by a 48 inch tall woven wire fence and 12 inch tall bromegrass. For over 90 years the road was faithful to early travelers and perhaps served as a quiet layover on the Underground Railroad's northbound siding. One can only imagine the images of horses and buggies rutting the roadbed's mud during March and November. Encores followed with the Model-T.

Like the road, and 11 percent of west-central Union County, the farm is composed of heavy clay soils. It's an area known locally as Bear Swamp, a land too soft when wet and too hard and dusty when dry. Early soil scientists concluded that the soil was formed as part of a former glacial lakebed. Today, more enlightened glacial geologist suggests that the soils are re-deposited glacial lake bottom scrapings. Deposits transported from who knows where, then surrendered, between the Broadway Moraine's Mill Creek and the Powell Moraine's Big Darby Creek by the transient Wisconsin Glacier.

Efforts to farm this land proved tedious. Seasonal wetness prohibited corn from ever being planted. A late variety of soybean, named Lincoln, was called upon for late-June to early-July planting. The boundary between poorly-drained Nappanee, and even wetter Paulding clay soil, was marked by stunted soybean plants with yellowed leaves. Farming was always done without chemicals.

The farm proved therapeutic for my dad, who with my mom and maternal grandmother, owned and operated a very successful family restaurant in Marysville. Dad's memories of farming as a boy were relived upon this farm. The aroma of fresh turned soil was omnipresent as the Golden Jubilee tugged a two bottom plow. This was modern farming. His father had relied upon Percheron horses named Dan and Belle to forge a living off of the land in adjacent Delaware County. To dad, this was real progress.

Sitting upon a huge horizontal limb of a white oak overlooking the field, I would share his pleasure. I watched his slow, but steady, advancement as he stole away from the hectic pace of a busy restaurant to be one with the land for a few brief hours each day.

As a young teen I did not understand many of farming's practices. I questioned the logic of battling clay that was either too wet or too dry. Nor did I understand why grassy waterways were not neater and wider. I unfailingly trusted that dad would do what was right whether I understood it or not.

In 1964, on one of my curiosity walks to the wilderness woods, I came upon a man with a transit in the extreme southwest corner. I discovered that he was siting the location of a proposed 8" diameter petroleum line from Indiana to a metered spigot somewhere else. Dad had sold the 50' wide easement without a quibble. I did not like the idea of a stranger making plans to cut and dig up these quiet woods. Sensing that I must be out of touch, I kept my opposition to the plan to myself. Today the pipe lay buried beneath a hump in the ground that mimics a shallow grave. Trees are kept removed on either side for 25'. Painted metal signs in the fencerow of the southeast to northwest swath announce an active buried pipeline, an epitaph for the former hickories that were born and raised here.

"One mustn't stand in the way of progress!" elders proclaimed.

I didn't agree and grew increasingly frustrated that I didn't understand what they obviously did.

Farm animals came to the farm, followed by more fence. We raised hobby cattle known as registered Red Polls. There was a foundered brown and white pony wrongly named "Bullet" that provided hours of slow riding.

From day-old ducklings, we reared 1200 white laying ducks in a low concrete block barn that measured 120' x 40'. The former owner built it for hogs that failed to return the favor. Each day we would gather 600 eggs and sell them to a hatchery in Mt. Healthy, Ohio for .96 cents a dozen, quite a price in 1966.

A series of events including severe electrical storms, power outages, and raiding fox sent the ducks into a frenzied molt. Egg production never recovered and the bedraggled ducks were sold for whatever used ducks are sold for.

In addition to big eggs, the ducks had produced valuable experiences and tons of saturated fertilizer. I had fond memories of spreading the soggy nutrients upon the fields. Each trip south across the hayfield would take me near the woods, a place where I always found happiness.

Life around and within was changing fast.

Farms, by their nature, sow independence into the warmest soul. I sensed such an individual emerging.

The farm now supported an FFA project of soybean production. Quite frankly I never understood the mumbo-jumbo record keeping of production soybeaning, but managed to do well in the 2 years that I engaged in it.

My real, or imagined, interest in farming ended by the time I was 17. This time-honored profession wasn't for me. However, my interest in the farm didn't end. It just moved to a different, albeit higher, plane.

I graduated from Marysville High School in 1970, though continued my education to sustain my 1-S student draft deferment. I felt no obligation to hike, hunt, and camp in the wooded wetlands of Southeast Asia.

At the farm another utility easement was being sought as Ohio Power planned to locate their 765Kv (765 thousand-volt) electric transmission line through our farm and west woods. Dad consented to the agreement and generous offer. The line began on the Ohio River in Gallipolis, Ohio and ran north, through the farm, to a substation in nearby Broadway, Ohio. The 200' wide easement completely removed many more trees from the increasingly fragmented west woods. In their place, giant galvanized steel towers dangled 3 gangs of 4 two-inch conductors. A quarter-mile spanned between the two towers on our farm. Tower 47, identified with an orange and black metal placard on the top support, sets upon a rise in the Millcreek Watershed field. One tower south, still on our farm, is The Big Darby Watershed. Between the sag, shadows of the humming lines are cast upon an inconspicuous ground moraine that divides watersheds.

I was dismayed and sickened by the immensity of this project. A crude haul road was constructed of fist-sized rocks where construction equipment rutted areas too wet for anything but mammals.

Today the noisy lines remain as do the static discharge shocks. Leftover haul road rocks continue to appear with each new season of frost heaving.

Progress had once again found our unresisting farm a favorable place to exploit. The only beneficiaries of this project, as far as I was able to determine, were shareholders of utility stocks. Their proxy vote did not enable them to see what their speculative investments were destroying.

A disturbing pattern of easement-taking was now in motion. It would not end.

Wedding bells and a career kept me very busy and away from the farm for the next three years. We lived in Richwood, a northern Union County town of 2,000 people, 17 miles to the northeast. Dad and brothers continued to plant the tired fields to monotonous soybeans in their spare time.

It was upon one of those slow trips north, ahead of the two bottom plow, that my dad discovered an undamaged Archaic Indian dovetail point of unknown chart. It cleanly rolled-out of the fresh-turned soil and softly landed in the neat furrow. He quickly stopped to pick it up. It had been 7,000-8,000 years since anyone had touched it. Thus, the farm revealed evidence of an earlier civilization. A secret once contained, was now exposed.

The farm contained many more secrets. In time, each would reveal themselves and add to its character and my attachment to this land.

In 1973 I would return to the farm for good and begin a mission and journey that would forever change my life.

My perspective of this world re-focused to reflect the reality I was living. Any and all healthy skepticism that was associated with the changing fortunes of "progress" would turn to cynicism. I had many more lessons to learn.

Our Great White Oak

The personality of a farm is often determined by the sum of its assets.

Those assets are usually the productive tamed fields and domestic farm animals that grow to turn a profit year after year. In time they become known as a grain, cattle, chicken, hog, or horse farms to neighbors, visitors, salespeople, and tax assessors.

Liabilities and losses are assigned to the forces of Nature that did not conspire to make the farmer even more money.

The character and soul of our farm is in its not-for-profit trees.

One tree in particular defines the farm's heritage, as well as its present, and its future.

White oaks (Quercus alba) find our farm most-acceptable in areas where they can keep their feet somewhat dry. A slight rise at the northwest corner of our woods is home to a picturesque white oak that measures 53" dbh. I call it our great white oak.

It is the near-geographic center of the farm. Apparently rejected by earlier sawyers because of a massive crotch at 6', the tree and its wide-spreading crown of 80' dwarf the first time visitor in stature and awe.

The tree seems as oversized today as it did when I was drawn to it at the age of 11. Visiting foresters have estimated its age at 250 years old... a seedling in the 1740's.

It does not seem like a tree, but rather a place. Its large lower horizontal limbs allowed easy climbing and a powerful view of the fields to the north and northwest. I spent many hours climbing the tree as a young boy. It may have well been the first place I found personal solitude in, a quiet place where perspectives could be experimented with. My wife, and our three sons and daughter, have all delighted in the pleasures of this kind and gentle giant. I still climb the tree on occasion, but have discovered that the ease of climbing up, then dropping down, are more of the things to gracefully surrender to youth.

It surely served as welcome shade for the workers who laid out, cleared, and ditched the old road in the early 1850's. The tree, already over a century old, was but 50 feet east, a distance not too far to eat lunch, or engage in a nap beneath. Can we deduce that today's highway workers are merely exercising traits pioneered by those who unhurriedly built the first roads?

So too must the now-extinct passenger pigeon have enjoyed its acorns and limbs of roost. How a species could go from billions-to-zero in one generation continues to amaze and sadden me. There are accounts of passenger pigeon flocks, numbering billions, taking hours to pass in the early and mid-1800's.

Perhaps the Carolina parakeets knew this oak as well; another secret that will never be revealed or shared.

The gregarious parakeets unintentionally disproved the "safety in numbers" theory of survival. It is wrong when empathy and compassion for one another results in extinction. The gentle birds would not disperse when shot at. Instead they assembled and seem to grieve over those recently shot. Shooters would then pick them off one by one. Wrongly persecuted, and now extinct, at least the birds were not his enemies—for Christians love their enemies.

I have seen deer bed down in the orchard grass beneath the oak's rounded canopy. I have watched yellow-shafted flickers raise families within the knotty and callused entrances of large limbs, locations where lesser limbs tried and failed. Fox squirrel have their own apartments with more than one way in and out.

December's lingering Eastern bluebirds have been seen using the flickers' summer homes as overnight roosts, an effective, but temporary retreat from the winter cold of 40 Degree North latitude. Does such bravery make stronger bluebirds, or does such carelessness eliminate daring bluebirds? I do not know.

The uppermost branch of the old oak serves as a rehearsal stage for the crimson male cardinal. He begins to practice his incomplete love song on those bright sunny mornings of late February. A song and purpose perfected by April 25th.

Any springy oak branch that the tufted-titmouse flits upon serves him. Weeks earlier than the cardinal, the energetic titmouse incessantly calls "Peter… Peter… Peter!" all day long. So do three others. There is now increased urgency in his call.

Unlike the cardinal, the titmouse is not content to stay in any one place long. It abruptly leaves the old oak, perhaps to return later today, or certainly tomorrow.

The patient knocking of January's downy woodpeckers is an attempt to rouse any insects that may be cuddled-up beneath the ledges of the bark's fissures. The Downies know full-well that the dormant insects will not be going anywhere soon. Theirs is an unhurried hunt. The nasal "yank-yank" of the restless white-breasted nuthatch is audible evidence of its herky-jerky snooping within the light gray plates and crevices of the old oak's bark. The spiraling-up of one tree trunk, after another, is the disciplined nature of the brown creeper. The trunk's 13' circumference challenges the creeper's navigational skills and appetite fulfillment.

This house of our great white oak serves many.

The Woods Nature Reserve, 1973

Global positioning satellites precisely identify the location of The Woods in terms of 40 Degrees; 14 Minutes; & 44.22 Seconds North Latitude @ 83 Degrees; 25 Minutes; & 02.19 Seconds West Longitude.

Topographic maps repeatedly confirm that our deciduous woodland floor is 1,040 feet above today's distant salty seas.

Directly below, through 152 feet of glacial till, a broad and deep river valley once snaked along the 450 million year old Silurian bedrock. Here flowed a tributary of the great pre-glacial Teays River. A continental course that crossed the eastern half of the United States from the headwaters of the Appalachian Mountains westward for 800 miles to southwestern Illinois. Successive glaciations filled the valley with till, including granitic erratic from the Canadian Shield. The late-great Wisconsin Glacier, 20,000-10,000 years ago, is responsible for the general terrain we know today.

These remain the established instrument readings and geology of the land area known as The Woods Nature Reserve located in Paris Township, County of Union, and State of Ohio.

Usually, such descriptions best serve to satisfy the requirements of deeds and titles. However, once one has become inextricably attached to the living land, its natural history details serve to validate and justify its proper place on Earth.

Important events in our lives are clearly remembered and often enhanced with the passage of time. Discoveries of special places are never forgotten, no matter how long one lives. Secrets once contained, are revealed to those prepared to embrace them.

A walk to the woods in July of 1973, following a short-lived early afternoon thunderstorm, forever changed my life. I had arrived by foot via the old earthen road that was growing waist-high in tall fescue, timothy, and hawthorns.

At the northwest corner of the woodlands, near the Great White Oak, pole hickories lined the top of the road's ditches. The enlarged lower leaflets were collecting the descending rain droplets from the normal-sized leaflets above. The droplets gained size and weight as the gently rolled-off the leaflets' serrate margins. Each resembled a transparent blue marble that reflected the now clear-blue sky. All around were the tranquil sounds of aggregate water droplets obeying the law of gravity. Hindered, though amended, by the palmate leaves of shagbark hickories, the raindrops' trip to the forest floor resembled a game of pinball. The brief thunderstorm had freshened the air, leaving me alone with God in a moment of perfect beauty and peacefulness. Ideas overfilled my head. This woodland would become a special place, a place to return to forever and ever.

There is much skepticism associated with the pronouncement of God-inspired events. Today, divine manifestations are often "accepted" by others with apologetic grins. Many Christians accept John's prophetic Book of Revelation as gospel—not the dubious writings of a very old mortal man, alone in exile, on the island of Patmos.

To this 21 year-old, The Woods Nature Reserve was God-inspired—period.

The farm's greatest secret, once contained, was now clearly revealed to me! Many more secrets would be exposed.

I returned each weekend to get a better feel for locations of trails in the woods. More than once I would find myself momentarily lost. North was found by turning an ear to the sound of persistent traffic along distant Rt. 33. It seemed that I always ended up in the same small clearing with the same large pin oak. Its lower dead limbs arched downward to touch the ground. One could easily walk upright around the tree's trunk and within an arboreal cage.

The clearing of fallen trees and volunteer hawthorns from the old roadbed seemed a fitting place to begin my lifelong project. A few years earlier, heavy rains had washed out the road where the waters of the ditches' confluence refused to squeeze through undersized culvert tiles. Two old 2 x 20 creosote boards were used to bridge the 5' gap in the clay roadbed.

The project was ambitious, though enjoyable for my wife, Teresa, and me.

Pioneering hawthorns, blackberry, and black raspberry canes were establishing themselves between the diseased and fallen elms. Ditches on either side served as important guides. Timothy, orchard grass, and tall fescue conspired to entangle the limbs of fallen trees. Often, it seemed as though the fallen trees' limbs were tied to the ground. Large piles of limbs and small trees were stacked in the middle of the roadbed every couple of hundred feet. They were burned before I discovered their value as wildlife brush piles. My simple 21" bow saw proved very effective in clearing the 59,125 sq. ft. of earthen roadbed succession. Looking south, the renewed grassy roadbed seemed to compliment the trunks and canopies of hickory, oak, and ash on either side.

Early trails were neatly marked by strips of worn out blue jeans provided by my wife. We tied them to the small limbs of hickory that weaved into larger oaks along the way. We even dreamed of building a home within the woods sometime in the near future.

I do not recall ever seeing a yellow-shafted flicker until I came to these woods. I was taken by their beauty, jungle-like calls, and bounding flight. I tried to learn as much as possible about the "yawker-birds," but soon discovered that their presence was all I needed. It was another secret contained, but now revealed.

By the winter of 1974 the roadbed led to a foot trail that took us to the now- familiar large pin oak in the partial clearing. We were now removing crowded trees and limbs with a chainsaw, bow saw, and pole pruner. Teresa, pregnant with our first son, would help me carry all this, plus fuel mix, bar oil, tools, and binoculars to the woods. Leaving our car in the barnyard drive, we walked across the frosty soybean stubble, to the frozen grassy roadbed, and onto the frost-heaved woodland litter of the woods.

Little by little, new-found features of the overgrown woods were becoming familiar. We sited new trails and pruned-away obstructing limbs.

We found a rise in the near middle of the woods and considered it the place to build a home. A huge rounded tip of granite, certainly from the Canadian Shield, surfaced about 10 inches high and 3 feet in diameter. Smoothed by rain and wind erosion, it was impossible to determine how much of this erratic lay buried. It would become a familiar landmark while hiking and served as a place to sit and reflect. Moss found it irresistible too.

This rise supported trees typical of uplands in white oaks, red oaks, and white ash. But the uneven acre also supported the flexible swamp white oak, pin oak, and black ash. Bitternut, mockernut, shellbark, and shagbark hickories, the mainstay of these woods, filled-in between.

By the winter of 1976, foot trails continued to softly network across the woods.

It was upon a sunny Saturday morning in January that I walked-up upon—within 10 feet of—a whitetail buck lying too comfortably alongside the trail. The trail clearing had provided a spot favorable for basking in bright and warm sunlight. My arms were filled with chainsaw; gas can, bar oil, bow saw, binoculars, and pole pruner as I watched it leap to its feet and bound away in one continuous motion. This was the very first deer I had ever seen at the farm, although tracks had announced an earlier presence. This unforgettable experience would be reason enough to return again and again to this special place on earth. It was another contained secret revealed to those prepared to see.

On a sunny day in May, I met up with my dad at an old apple tree along the road. In full blossom, its fragrance was intoxicating. He was walking along the edge of the still unplanted field, just west of the old roadbed. I was walking the fresh green roadbed, side-stepping dandelions, in search of colorful northbound warblers. Our eyes met at the same moment, even though neither knew the other was anywhere around. We talked and enjoyed the beautiful spring afternoon.

To this day, I recall the experience as vividly as if it were yesterday, a moment in time that I will never forget and forever cherish.

In July of 1978, Teresa and I completed the winding 1402 foot long trail that resembled a large distorted question mark. It led past hickory, ash, and oak to that spot in the woods where our new home would be. Selective clearing continued upon the woodland rise for two more years. The perfect days of October brought fall colors to their peak against clear-blue skies. The winter snows came quietly to the woods. For the first time in my life I was able to hear the sound of snow falling all around me. Friends would give a sideward glance when I related such revelations, but I had heard snow falling. I would hear it again and again upon subsequent journeys into our serene winter woods.

This secret, once contained, was now revealed to anyone prepared to listen.

The silence and remoteness of the location proved too powerful for any further consideration as a home site. This area would remain quiet woods unto itself.

The finished trail would remain the primary trail of The Woods. We named it "The Trail of '78."

On the early cold morning of February 17, 1979, at the age of 53, my ailing dad progressed into eternal life. His chronic heart problems were over. The greatest man I had ever known was no longer around. I still had a million more questions to ask dad, none greater than how a man with such a kind and gentle heart, could have a "bad" heart?

Perhaps, he knew that the greatest gift he ever gave me was the opportunity to enjoy the farm and all of the Nature within. In prayer, I continue to thank him to this day.

In some quiet night's dream, I want to meet up with dad again in May at the old apple tree and ask if he is well pleased with what I have done with his farm. I miss dad so much.

Mom became the surviving owner of the farm, and entrusted decisions for its use to me and my brother, Ron—who now lived in the farmhouse.

Farming continued with new renters and contracts each year. Each brought bigger and better equipment, but the yields declined. Like dad's, the hearts of the fields seemed too weak to continue in their present form. The large equipment was unable to reach the square corners of the fields. Here sedges and rushes were succeeding. I saw a hint and promise of better things to come.

On August 13, 1979, we purchased a 20' x 24" diameter aluminum drainage pipe to cross the washed-out roadbed of years' earlier. Nearby rocks were gathered to weight the tile pipe in place. Use of my father-in-law's old pick-up enabled me to haul a total of 9 tons of fist-sized rocks.

They were free for the hauling because they were mistakenly delivered to a friend's lot in town. Many trips later the road was whole again.

On October 1, 1979, I applied to The Ohio Department of Transportation (ODOT) for a permit to install a drive entrance linking the fenced-in old abandoned road with blacktopped two lanes U.S. Rt. 33. Written permission was asked of, and granted by, the Paris Township Trustees on November 13, 1979. Such pressing official acts served to fill the trustees' monthly agenda and guaranteed an audience of at least one.

Construction of the entrance began on December 15, 1979. The following week-end I cut open the fencerow, installed an old gate, and raked-out the details. The old roadbed was now open for the comings and goings of private, not public, landowners.

By 1981 we selected another site at the thin clearing of the first foot trail's old pin oak. With few young hickories yet to clear, this site was closer to the old roadbed and an open field to the north. Access would be easier and disturbance to the woodlands would be less. This site would feature a pre-cut log home—just like the models we visited.

Trail-making within the woods enabled us to discover the walking stick, puff balls, Mayapples, and red-bellied woodpeckers. Increasingly more secrets, once contained, were revealed as necessary. Work was always rewarded with some new insight into Nature. The full moon casts it light upon a billion leaves in the summer, and a million stark branches in the winter. The silvery-blue light that reaches the woodland floor, a color that one can feel, seems to make the nocturnal woods a sacred and holy place.

There was now a perimeter trail linking-up to the crooked diagonal trails throughout the woods. In the early spring of 1983, my wife and our three young sons placed a routered sign near the giant old white oak proclaiming this, the location of the God-inspired: "The Woods Nature Reserve." It featured Henry David Thoreau's verse of why he went to Walden woods in July of 1845.

Bewildered by the sheer number of small hickories in the woods, I sought free technical assistance on managing the woodland stand. On March 18, 1983, I met with Jim Bartlett, service forester—Ohio Department of Natural Resources (ODNR)—Division of Forestry on-site at the woods. We discussed a forest management plan that would benefit wildlife as well as the trees. Jim showed me the tiny red flowers of the American hazelnut that grew for twenty feet on the east side of the old abandoned road near the ditch.

Here, in the middle of March, I learned of a plant with far more confidence of spring's return than me. Each March 18th I return to the hazels to look for, and find, the bright and tiny red flower of the anxious spring. It transforms into a delicious nut that is eaten prematurely by chipmunks and fox squirrels. After all, anything would be sweeter than the bitter cache of last year's tannin-rich red oak acorns.

This was another one of the old farm's beautiful secrets… once concealed, but now revealed.

The farm had changed noticeably in the past 21 years. The springtime's water now flowed unimpeded in ditches. The rejuvenated roadbed was again whole and open from The Woods to Rt. 33. A timber stand improvement project plan and a wildlife management plan were being written for The Woods and the farm by The Ohio Department of Natural Resources. The clear cuts of a pipeline and a power line easement detracted from the vista, but there were quiet new trails in The Woods to walk and enjoy this Easter weekend. While others flocked to the Churches of their choice, I was worshipping in solitude at The Woods. Many know the House of God, but I know where God lives!

Gone were the junk piles, stumps, and catalpas that defined the distant northwest barnyard lot. In their place stood the transplanted old farmhouse where my brother lived. The tall cottonwood now served as a front yard tree, not a barnyard tree. The disoriented old house had been moved from its original location near the U.S. Rt. 33 right of way with taxpayers' dollars. The Ohio Department of Transportation (ODOT) determined that it would sit too close to a hastily planned widening project for U.S. Rt. 33. The controversial and highly unpopular project would serve the increased traffic from Marysville to Honda's new motorcycle plant, six miles west. The who's-who of local governments, irate citizens, and ODOT officials wrestled with plans to widen two-lane U.S. Rt. 33 to three or four lanes. All knew that such plans would never work. Blind progress had brought too much vehicle traffic to this unprepared rural area. Ego-rich state and local officials had greedily thrown out the welcome mat for a foreign-based corporation to cross. Not only did Honda use the mat, but they took the threshold and door. They changed the locks and started calling all of the future shots. They needed an expanded highway, and they needed it now. They had even bigger and better plans for the greedy community to droll over.

While the farm's white silo remained, the decrepit wooden barn next to it was now gone. So were the sagging gates and rusty water trough that I had filled so many times.

Mom had recently received another vague form-letter from The Ohio Department of Transportation (ODOT). It stated that general data was being collected throughout west-central Union County for inventory and review. If crucial monies became available for new highway construction, the preliminary data would already be known. I asked a former classmate, then a neighboring Allen Township Trustee, his knowledge of any proposed new highway plan. He told me that the early and indefinite plans he had seen would go considerably south of our farm and west of his nearby land.

Any apprehensions of losing land to a new highway were quickly allayed. After all, his assurances were based upon the latest inside information that township trustees receive and enjoy.

The Relocation of US Route 33 vs. Nature

On Thursday July 28, 1983, The Ohio Department of Transportation (ODOT) held a public meeting in the little theater of Marysville High School. They were to present plans for the long-awaited Relocation of U.S. Route 33 between Marysville and Honda's assembly plant in western Union County. The proposed new highway would fulfill promises the State of Ohio made to Honda for locating here.

We attended the meeting out of curiosity. We just wanted to see just how far away the proposed highway would be constructed. There were local and county officials, newspaper reporters, and the Columbus-based CBS Affiliate—WBNS 10TV's Eyewitness News present to see and feel the public's reaction to this major news story affecting rural Union County.

It was crowded. There were monotone speeches from ODOT officialdom introducing the 4 design alternatives being presented for the public to review, discuss, and decide upon in the coming months.

Edging forward through the murmuring crowd, I made it to the tall drawings in front by turning sideways and excusing myself for bumping into people in the stuffy auditorium.

It took a few seconds until I found the general area of the farm on the drawings. In a split second I wondered why the farm was even on the maps, in less time than that I saw the new highway highlighted in a broad bright pink band diagonally-perfect through our woods and farm!

This couldn't be. I grabbed the back of my head with both hands and dropped to my knees to get a closer look. Disbelief and panic set in. I called for my wife, mom, and brother. "It goes right through the farm. The Woods will be sliced in half!" I griped.

Others cautioned me that there were four alternatives and that perhaps the farm would be avoided. "No!" I said, "The farm is the only common link to all four alternatives!" No matter what, the farm was about to be destroyed.

I had to get outside for fresh air. I was livid, angry, and bitter. I was cursing ODOT and Honda under my breath.

Outside, near the school's entrance, a line had formed to tell the TV reporter and cameraman just how the highway would affect them.

There were the typical Reponses of concern. Some said the highway would take a part of their soybean field, or the highway would be too close to their house.

The reporter pretended to have empathy for their concerns, but it seemed like so many other similar interviews he had conducted. It came time for me to answer how the highway would affect me.

I told him that the State of Ohio was about to destroy our Nature Reserve. He was taken aback, and asked me to repeat what I just said. He became alert and interested. He asked for more details. I asked them to leave the meeting and follow us to The Woods to see firsthand what ODOT was planning to destroy.

They checked their watches and said: "Let's go!"

It was still daylight as we arrived at The Woods 5 minutes later. Shafts of orange sunlight shot through openings in the leafy canopy. The videographer was shooting all kinds of woodland trail and clearing footage as the reporter took quick notes and asked rapid-fire questions about our long work in these beautiful woods.

There was an intense interest in his eyes and voice. By 9:00 PM they were leaving for their news room in Columbus—40 minutes away. This story would break on the 10TV's 11:00 PM News that night.

The lead tease and news story that night was ODOT's plan to destroy The Woods Nature Reserve with the Relocation of U.S. Rt. 33.

The green woods, in its late July fullness, were tranquil and serene. This was no place for a re-located 4-lane limited access highway.

The broadcast ended with the reporter asking:

"Which will hold more sway: The will of the State, or the dreams of a family?"

Two more broadcasts would follow in the coming months.

The following 133 day chronology involved countless hours of writing over 200 letters on my wife's manual typewriter. Our family wrote to relatives, individuals, government agencies, natural resource organizations, elected officials, strangers and friends.

Those friends apparently wrote nearly as many letters.

My discoveries included disappointment and frustration.

In the end, fulfillment was realized as The Woods were preserved from certain destruction.

It was an experience that opened my eyes to how government and elected officials really operate.

They play it safe. All around me people were playing it safe!

Local Couple Fights State To Keep Property

With more and more instances of every-day living becoming hurried along in a concrete jungle, one local family is looking to escape it all through communing with nature. However, if the State of Ohio has its way, that back-to-the-basics way of life could be threatened.

The State of Ohio wants to re-locate U.S. 33, west of Marysville, but they want to construct the new highway through the Woods Nature Reserve, a site which the John Rockenbaugh family, 134 E. Ottawa St., wants to build their next home, a log cabin.

The Woods Nature Reserve is a 20-acre private woods of mixed hardwoods, located on the farm owned by John's parents, Catherine and the late Dorance Rockenbaugh. It is located two miles west of Marysville on U.S. 33.

At a July 28 Ohio Dept. of Transportation (ODOT) meeting in Marysville, a new U.S. 33 was proposed, which according to Rockenbaugh, would diagonally slice the Woods and the farm in half and would cut a 300 feet wide by 1,305 feet long swath through pure woodland. Nearly nine acres of the woods would be destroyed. Rockenbaugh added the southern half of the Woods would be "landlocked," while the remaining northern half would be rendered "useless."

The state of course would pay for the land, but Rockenbaugh wants to keep the nature reserve as it is, with its full beauty.

Rockenbaugh, along with his wife, Teresa, has taken many steps in an attempt to stop the re-location of the highway through the family property. They have contacted state, county and ODOT officials about the matter and have taken many persons on tours of the Woods, including Don South, a representative for Cong. Mike DeWine and members of the news media.

Originally, U.S. 33 was to be widened to four lanes at its present site, however, a group of residents along the highway was able to stall that move. After that measure was stalled, ODOT reportedly revealed plans in July to re-locate the highway through the Woods.

Rockenbaugh is upset over what the state is trying to do. "The Woods Nature Reserve is the direct result of a truly God-inspired idea and with a lot of hard work we (the family) have cleared the area for the reserve. We have a lot of wildlife living here as well as much plant life. Teresa and I have taught our three sons that the ideals of the Woods are what life and real living really are. It is completely impossible to imagine the Woods beneath the blades of a 'murderous' bulldozer!"

The Rockenbaughs want more input as to where feelings lie on this matter.

They hope they can learn more about it at a public meeting, scheduled for 7 p.m. tonight at Benjamin Logan High School in Zanesfield.

John and Teresa Rockenbaugh of Richwood are shown at the staked site of their log cabin at the Woods Nature Reserve, located off U.S. 33, west of Marysville. The site is being threatened by the proposed re-location of the highway.

He fought for slice of nature

By Robert W. Reiss
Dispatch Staff Reporter

MARYSVILLE, Ohio — The opening of a four-lane section of Rt. 33 yesterday drew applause from government and business officials, but not from John Rockenbaugh.

He has waged war with the state for five years, trying to stop the highway relocation.

The opening comes 11 years after the state promised the new road for Honda, which built a motorcycle and auto manufacturing plant here.

THE RELOCATED section of Rt. 33, which stretches 8.4 miles west of Marysville to the Logan County line, was opened to traffic yesterday, 27 months after ground was broken. It cost $35.1 million.

Bernard B. Hurst, director of the Ohio Department of Transportation, said the two-lane Rt. 33 will be widened to four lanes west from where the new section of highway ends to link it with the four-lane bypass at Bellefontaine.

He said the 16 mile extension will be started in either 1990 or 1991.

While local officials were happy that the new Rt. 33 is finished, Rockenbaugh invited anyone interested to view the damage he says has been done to his private nature preserve.

Dispatch photo by Ro

The Rockenbaughs, from left, Timothy, Tracie, Teresa and John, on the prese

Rockenbaugh's parents bought a farm on the southside of the original section of Rt. 3 in 1962. His father, until his death in 1979, farmed part of the land. The rest was woods and grassland.

ROCKENBAUGH'S mother, Catherine, still owns the farm but does not live on it. Rockenbaugh has worked at a local auto dealership for 18 years.

After his father's death part of the farmland was rented But Rockenbaugh set aside 41 acres, including the woods, for a nature preserve.

When the state announced plans for the new highway that would cut through the preserve, he started a letter-writing campaign and appeared at public hearings to protest.

The state appropriated seven acres and paid Mrs. Rockenbaugh $16,375. The highway cut off an additional seven acres of woodlands to which there is no access except through another farmer's fields. The state offered to pay $1,200 for the cut-off land, but the Rockenbaughs refused.

The new highway runs along one side of John Rockenbaugh's

remaining 22 acres of nature preserve. He is the noise, pollution and harming the plants an

HE MADE one con the new highway. He let a contractor remove a field in return for six-acre pond, built to Conservation Service s

John Rockenbaugh wife, Teresa, had pl build a house on the now they aren't sure to build where they trucks going by day an

John Rockenbaugh, standing with his wife, Teresa, points out where U.S. 33 would cross their "Woods" if the highway is relocated according to one proposal under consideration. The Rockenbaughs have turned their land into a nature preserve, and hope to prevent the state from taking any of it for the highway. He made the 33 sign in the photo.

(J-T Photo)

Couple Fights To Preserve
Natural Area Near U.S. 33

By LANA WETTERMAN

When ODOT displayed plans to build an alternate route for U.S. 33 east of Marysville rather than widen the existing one, some people whose homes would've been perilously close to the widened highway breathed sighs of relief. For two of their neighbors, however, it seemed the problems were just beginning.

John and Teresa Rockenbaugh are two of those neighbors. Although they and their young sons live in Richwood right now, they hope to eventually build their dream home - a log cabin - in a fully preserved 20-acre tract of woodland located opposite Cradler-Turner Rd. on U.S. 33.

They fear, however, that transportation officials are leaning toward a route for the new U.S. 33 which will, by those plans, running the highway right across their little reserve.

They are trying to prove their land's value as a natural, preserved habitat deserves to be saved. Just moving the proposed route "a few thousand feet" either way, they say, will save the vast majority of the woods and would cause less serious laceration to neighboring fields as well.

When they saw the proposed new routes for U.S. 33 which were displayed at a public meeting in July sponsored by ODOT. "We saw it was going right down the middle of our land," Rockenbaugh said.

The 20-acre parcel is part of a 90-acre farm purchased by Rockenbaugh's father, the late Dorrance "Rocky" Rockenbaugh. "It's in the family," said Mrs. Rockenbaugh. "It's always been someplace where we could bring our family, and we always dreamed that one day we'd have a home here."

In the past 10 years, both have put in many hours to make the woodland, which they call "The Woods Nature Reserve," a place where their families could "live the good life" side by side with nature. In the meantime, they, their three sons and their friends and relatives have enjoyed many good times in the relative quiet and seclusion of the back-to-nature setting, and have come to look upon it as a welcome retreat.

Rockenbaugh, although an automotive mechanics specialist by trade, is an avid naturalist in spirit. Together, he and his wife have made the deepest nooks of the woods accessible to nature-conscious visitors by adding 1½ to 2 miles of trails. Strolling along those

the site — bluebird houses at regular intervals, rail fences made from some of the underbrush they cleared, benches at rest stops and salt blocks they placed for the deer.

They hacked the choking underbrush out of some areas to enhance natural clearings, and purposely left it in others where it serves as homes and hiding places for rabbits, squirrels, raccoons and other creatures. They released ringnecked pheasants on the land in conjunction with the Department of Natural Resources pheasant restoration program.

"You can see deer here at any time," Rockenbaugh said. Screech owls and at least one barred owl, as well as several varieties of woodpeckers also share the area.

The flora is at least as varied and abundant as the fauna. A 300-year-old white oak and shagbark hickories are among the oldest residents, sharing the area with ironwood trees, varieties of cherry, locust, wildflowers like goldenrod and New England asters, and wild blackberries. "There's a lot of big trees back here," said Mrs. Rockenbaugh, "and a lot of trees that just want to get big."

So far, their cabin consists of some boundary stakes set in a clearing in the middle of parcel. The Rockenbaughs hope their home gets beyond that stage, but lately, those stakes have been joined by others which mark the outer boundaries of the proposed highway.

When they approached ODOT about it, the Rockenbaughs said they were told the area would be the subject of an "environmental study." That study, Rockenbaugh reported, consisted of a series of aerial photographs taken from a few hundred feet above the woods.

They asked for a more indepth investigation, pointing out that there are some things aerial photos just don't show - things like fox dens beneath the roots of an ancient tree, or the thickets where Rockenbaugh has seen does hide their fawns.

This morning, biologists from ODOT's department of environmental studies were to make personal visits to The Woods to do a more indepth study of the area. The Rockenbaughs have also asked for support from other quarters, including Cong. Mike DeWine's office. They hope that what the biologists and others see will make them think twice before putting a highway down the middle.

"This is just no place for a highway, in my opinion," Rockenbaugh said.

The proposed rerouting of U.S. 33 will be the topic of another public meeting slated for Tuesday at 7 p.m. in Benjamin Logan High School, Zanesfield.

Chronology: July 29, 1983-January 17, 1984

July 29, 1983

    Went to The Woods with Teresa and our three sons, Brodie, Caleb, and Timothy; Ages 9, 6, and 1. We measured where proposed U.S. Rt. 33 would slice through. As expected, the centerline was very near the peaceful Trail of '78.

    Reality was upon us.

August 2, 1983

    My oldest son, Brodie, and I began to mark the trail that would follow the near centerline of the proposed highway. It would become known as The No-33 Trail. We worked in the rain and by nightfall the rough trail, 1305' long, was laid out. It was a trail that would become a victory for Nature, and a loss for ODOT.

August 5, 1983

    Wrote to the ODOT District 6 Deputy Director, the Paris Township Trustees, and the Union County Commissioners stating our concerns with the proposed highway's alignment and asking for their time to come to The Woods for an on-site visit and tour.

August 11, 1983

    An ODOT District 6 engineer called me at work to arrange an on-site tour for Tuesday August 16th with the deputy director.

August 15, 1983

    The Union County Commissioners responded with the following:

> *"We were unaware of your efforts to create such a preserve. Perhaps this is the key to your problem. Since the preserve is a privately operated program, we feel you will have to take the steps to make it known to ODOT and the EPA to have the environmental impact become a significant factor in selecting a new location for U.S. Rt. 33."*

August 16, 1983

We met with three ODOT Officials, and our friend Dave Secor, at The Woods. ODOT officials included: the deputy director, an engineer, and an environmental specialist. The deputy director's first question was: "Is there any snakes in there?"

I asked many questions, but ODOT made no commitments to anything. They did say that if this were state land, they couldn't touch it.

August 17, 1983

Went to visit the Soil Conservation Service Office in Marysville to see District Conservationist and friend, Jim Rush, to ask suggestions for help. He wasn't optimistic about any chances for re-routing the plan. He advised me to contact the Assistant Director of ODOT since he once worked for the Union County Engineer's Office.

August 17, 1983

Wrote a letter to the active Ohio Environmental Council asking for help. I would never receive a response or acknowledgment of letter received.

August 18, 1983

Wrote sincere letter to Ohio Governor Celeste seeking his attention, via certified mail-return receipt requested.

September 14, 1983

The Paris Township Trustees met and sent the following letter:

"At the Paris Township Trustee meeting held last night your letter [Aug. 5th] was read. At this time the Trustees are taking your letter under advisement and will look further into the matter. Thank you for your input and letter."

September 19, 1983

ODOT's Bureau of Environmental Services biologist called from Columbus to arrange an on-site meeting at The Woods on Friday morning September 23rd.

September 21, 1983

Met with Ohio's 7th District Congressman Mike DeWine's District Representative at The Woods along with a Union County Commissioner and reporters from The Marysville Journal Tribune and The Richwood Gazette.

September 23, 1983

Met on-site with two ODOT wildlife biologists from state office in Columbus. They listened and asked a few questions. They took no notes. These were very disinterested biologists who acted bored and offended to be here.

I questioned the real motive of wildlife biologists working for ODOT.

September 26, 1983

A front page news story, with picture, appeared in The Marysville Journal Tribune giving our perspective. My wife's following quote seemed to say it best:

"There are a lot of big trees back here, and a lot of trees that just want to get big!"

September 27, 1983

Ohio's 87th House District State Representative called to offer support.

September 27, 1983

The second ODOT Public Meeting was held at Benjamin Logan High School in Logan County. Our efforts to date had not resulted in any design change or re-routing of the new highway.

WBNS -10TV Eyewitness News was there again to report on a follow-up to the July 28 news broadcast. The 11:00 O'clock news featured the deputy director saying that:

"...We are sensitive to their plight... but we have a highway to build."

The reporter ended his story with the continuing statement and question:

"The State appears pretty adamant about its plans, and The Rockenbaughs adamant about fighting them."

"Now we will see what holds more sway, the will of The State or the dreams of a family?

—Mike Horwitz, Eyewitness News, Marysville."

September 28, 1983

A front page story and photo appeared in The Richwood Gazette giving our perspective of this battle. In conclusion I stated:

"We have a lot of wildlife living here as well as plant life. Teresa and I have taught our three sons that the ideals of The Woods are what life and real living really are. It is completely impossible to imagine The Woods beneath the blades of a 'murderous' bulldozer!"

September 30, 1983

Our dear friend, student minister, naturalist, biologist, and former U.S. Parks Service employee, Dave Secor, called the Governor's Office to complain about ODOT's insensitivity to our plight. Dave was told by aides that the office would get back to him in five working days. Dave was livid over the deputy director's comments.

October 3, 1983

Received a hand-written post card from a local realtor expressing:

"John & Teresa,

Keep up the fight! We've destroyed about as much of wildlife in the name of 'Progress' as America can stand.

Good luck.

Dan Anderson,

Richwood Reality"

October 3, 1983

Dave Secor called Teresa to say that the Governor's Office called him and said that a meeting will be set up with the Governor and Honda officials soon.

This "promise," made to a student minister, would be denied weeks later by the governor's staffers.

October 3, 1983

A state reporter from The Columbus Dispatch dropped by at work to ask me questions. He had already gone to the farm on his own. His story will appear in the next few days.

October 3, 1983

This fiery letter was received on official Ohio Department of Transportation stationery from the ODOT District 6 Deputy Director in Delaware, Ohio:

"I can certainly understand the frustration and disgust you must feel for the Department of Transportation and our plans to relocate U.S. Route 33 through your land. However, you stated that the proposed alternates were politically motivated. I take PERSONAL offense to this statement being that I am involved in the planning. You have been afforded an opportunity to have my staff and I, and the staff of the Bureau of Environment Services to visit your land in order to get a firsthand look at 'The Woods' which I think you deserve. You have notified the media and other individuals about your plight in order to seek their help; again this is your right.

"This time, however Mr. Rockenbaugh, you have taken a posture lower than the animals you are seeking to save, and I might add, you are wrong."

October 3, 1983

This condensed letter was written and sent to every ODOT contact we had made. It reflects our weariness, exasperation, and remaining hope. The nasty preceding letter from the District 6 Deputy Director crossed in the mail.

> *10/3/83*
>
> *"John & Teresa Rockenbaugh Brodie, Caleb, & Timothy 134 East Ottawa Street Richwood, Ohio 43344*
>
> *Perhaps Man's last superhighway will lead him to a ticket-selling city zoo to see such wild game as the cottontail rabbit, the red fox, or by chance a ring-neck pheasant; or to a sterile state park for the botany study of the endangered species known as hickory, oak, and walnut… but never again a Mayapple!*
>
> *John & Teresa Rockenbaugh"*

August, 1983

To Each and to All,

The Woods Nature Reserve taught new things to some of your people and served to bore others—it appears.

To the people not involved with ODOT, the public, The Woods are a beautiful place to walk, learn, relax, and enjoy!

It is impossible to explain the real value and importance of The Woods without a visit.

We firmly believed that on-site visits by ODOT, especially ODOT's Bureau of Environmental Services, would instill excitement and appreciation for our project.

Thus far, it appears we have only bored you with just another woodlot in the corridor of the proposed relocated U.S. Rt. 33.

To you, perhaps The Woods is just another parcel to walk through or examine from an aerial photo—then check-off on a yellow sheet of legal pad paper!

There is something suspect with a system that operates too much in dollars and ignores innocent Nature and wildlife.

This errant highway proposal is an effort to fulfill promises to a foreign land investor that is ducking behind the facade of Honda/U.S.A.! We hear legitimate complaints about losing land to "foreign investors," but there is more than land involved in this loss, there is the destruction of habitat for Nature and wildlife.

While the Japanese were mercilessly blowing the life out of Pearl Harbor, The Woods Nature Reserve area was a State of Ohio Game Refuge, administered by The Ohio Department of Conservation. "Hunting is Unlawful," read the rusty sign we found on the western border of The Woods.

We realize that the sociological aspect of this project is your primary concern. Somewhere, somehow, and at a time in the future (if not now), the ecological aspects MUST be equal, if not greater in importance!

The Woods Nature Reserve, being a truly God-inspired project, does not deserve this devastating highway project. We have the faith of a single grain of mustard seed that this proposed project will not destroy The Woods!

We are confident in faith that the long hours spent clearing Abandoned Road 141 by hand; of creating thousands of feet of Nature trails; of designing succession clearings and providing approved habitat, will play a part in re-routing this misplaced "common link."

The countless hours of dreams and plans—of work and play—deciding to be a part of Nature, NOT apart from Nature, will not be in vain!

At what point does an impersonal public project, for a foreign-based corporation, take precedence over an active God-inspired project of preserving Nature and wildlife by private owners, using private funds on private lands?

Why must the people supporting government always have to make room when the government says: "MOVE!"?

We have been the self-appointed protector of Nature and wildlife, wildlife under the jurisdiction of the state. The same state that wishes to pave-over and through an innocent area.

What do we do for the living wildlife that will be displaced by this proposed highway project?

Do we send out a road crew to scrape-up a confused white tail deer who used to cross this area when it was a safe, natural, and inviting woodland cover?

Perhaps we will just let the buzzards soar down and pick at its carcass? This would be more natural—but then the hungry buzzards would be in jeopardy from oncoming traffic!

The Woods co-exists in the natural order of things! U.S. Rt. 33, as proposed, cannot offer this natural order.

We deeply appreciated ODOT's visits to The Woods. At no time did we ever feel that there was genuine concern for our project by ODOT officials.

We would have loved to have shown the difference between a "walk'n stick" (Carya ovata) and a walkingstick (Diapheromera femorata). We could have set upon a bench in The Woods and discussed the differences in leaf margins of the Hawthorns (Crataegous spp.) Perhaps a scattered pile of blue jay feathers would have led to a conversation of just what predator was responsible and how it might have happened!

We might well have talked of the serious plight of the Eastern bluebird and the prospects of the next year's residents. Walking past the goldenrod, we sense the aroma of it when bent or broken. We discuss how its heavy pollen is wrongly blamed for causing hay fever.

Standing beneath the 250 year-old white oak, at the entrance of The Woods, we can only imagine what was taking place in history when a squirrel buried, or just dropped, an extra acorn from that year's slim crop.

We could have walked to the large pin oak located at The Oaks clearing and found an owl pellet from a barred owl—a permanent resident of The Woods. Dissecting this pellet would have revealed what seeds a deer mouse had eaten prior to its sudden death beneath the talons of this skilled hunter of the night. The story of the balance of Nature is told in tightly-packed owl pellets!

In the middle of The Woods is the stage where the uncommon green dragon (Arisaema dracontious) plays out its fruiting role in a few short months. A walk to the margins of The Woods would have led us to the many black raspberry patches that provide the tasty fruit from which my wife, Teresa, made pies last July.

Along these same borders, one could see and hear the cardinals darting among the understory trees.

Walking about any of the interior trails would lead one past the whirring music of crickets. We find it nearly impossible to pinpoint the location of this energetic insect.

Let it be winter, and one could hear snow falling upon these same trails!

In the spring, the beginning, we could walk the woodland floor adorn in a mass of ankle-deep blue flowers.

In the summer light of June, fire pinks (Silene virginica) stand as signal flares against the green curtain of hickory and oak leaves. We watch as a scarlet tanager ignites the quivering leaves of the Eastern cottonwood with its no-nonsense flight through them.

In the fall, we listen and watch as a squadron of gathered-up blue jays flies reconnaissance over the golden-leaved tree tops. They stop to party at a cluster of clinging acorns—spooking a sleepy screech owl from its roost in another tree 75 yards away. Before the little owl can resettle, it is intercepted by "Blue Jay Leader." In time the raucous squawks of harassment wear-out as the jays continue on-course for some more "good times" in the still warm October sun.

In winter, the snow-laden landscape of night is bright as day beneath the soft illumination of the January Full Moon.

These are the event that we would have liked to have shown The Ohio Department of Transportation, but never felt that this was of their interest.

If we could somehow begin to explain the intrinsic beauty and immense importance of this Nature Reserve (and you could understand and see our very point), there would not be a highway going through this innocent woodland!

Nature is how we learn of God's love for all creation! We have prayed that The Ohio Department of Transportation will find a way to avoid this property. In God We Trust!

If we could make each of you lay down your T-squares, slide rules, standards of design, and aerial photos to walk The Woods—on your own for a sunny day and moonlit night—you would find a proper place for this highway we are sure!

(Please do not ever throw this away! Please! Thank You!)

 Sincerely from our hearts,

 Mr. & Mrs. John Rockenbaugh & Family

October, 1983

The Columbus Dispatch reporter called me at home to finish up some questioning. I told him that the Governor had promised a meeting and that things were shaping up. He reminded me: "You have taken on a formidable opponent."

October 5, 1983

The ODOT District 6 Deputy Director called me at work, on my lunch hour, to re-state his displeasure and personal offense to my suggestion of political motivation in the design of the highway. I told him that I didn't care what ODOT thought.

October 5, 1983

Wrote a letter, in hope, to The Nature Conservancy seeking their help.

October 6, 1983

The Columbus Dispatch story appeared today and stated in part:

> *"Rockenbaugh believes his efforts to make a nature preserve where deer roam freely, foxes build dens, and birds and other small game abound, should affect the decision.*
>
> *Rockenbaugh since has received word the governor will meet with him sometime."*

October 7, 1983

Ohio's 87th, House District State Representative called again to say the Columbus Dispatch story of 10/6/83 was just great and wants to visit The Woods on Saturday, October 15.

October 7, 1983.

A letter was given to a governor's staff worker for hand-delivery directly to the governor.

October 8, 1983

Wrote late night letters to The National Audubon Society and The National Wildlife Federation desperately seeking their help.

October 9, 1983
   Wrote to The American Forestry Association seeking their help.

October 10, 1983
   ODOT called our friend, Dave, on behalf of The Governor's Office, to arrange a meeting with Dave at ODOT state headquarters in Columbus on Monday, October 17, 1983.

October 15, 1983
   Our State Representative met us at The Woods for a tour and discussion for two hours. She took many questions back to her office for ODOT to answer.

October 18, 1983
   Received a letter from our state representative with this rather insensitive summary:

   "I hate to say it because I know how strongly you feel about this particular piece of land but, if you are still dissatisfied in December with the route, the money (from a taking) could be invested in another piece of wooded property."

October 20, 1983
   The following conclusion came from the administrative assistant for special projects in the governor's office:

   "The Governor's Office must support the determination of the ODOT Director. A copy of this letter will be forwarded to the Director and a request made that he limit the use of The Woods as much as prudently possible."

October 21, 1983
   Received a hurried-up letter from The Ohio Chapter of The Sierra Club referring me to some area activists that never acknowledged receipt of our letters.

October 26, 1983—November 2, 1983
   Staged a massive letter-writing blitz, with friends, to hit officials between these dates.

October 31, 1983
   Sent a letter to the Ohio State University School of Natural Resources—Environmental Education Section seeking enlightenment, but getting no response.

October 31, 1983
   Sent a two-page letter to Honda's Kiyoshi Kawashima asking his help in re-routing the new highway. Receipt of letter was never acknowledged.

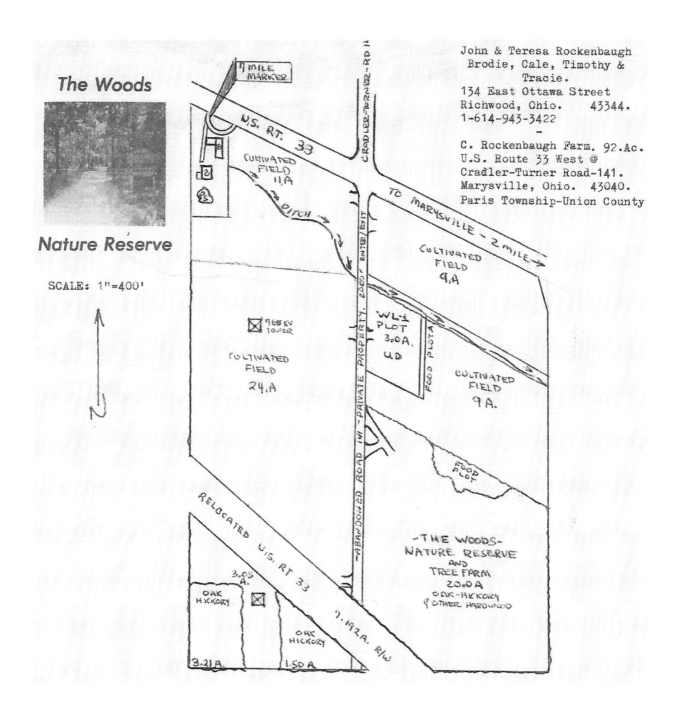

The Woods

Nature Reserve

SCALE: 1"=400'

N

John & Teresa Rockenbaugh
Brodie, Cale, Timothy &
Tracie.
134 East Ottawa Street
Richwood, Ohio.   43344.
1-614-943-3422

C. Rockenbaugh Farm. 92.Ac.
U.S. Route 33 West @
Cradler-Turner Road-141.
Marysville, Ohio. 43040.
Paris Township-Union County

1 MILE MARKER

U.S. RT. 33

CRADLER-TURNER RD.

TO MARYSVILLE - 2 MILE

CULTIVATED FIELD 11.A

DITCH

CULTIVATED FIELD 9.A

765 KV TOWER

CULTIVATED FIELD 24.A

200' ENTER EXIT

ABANDONED ROAD 141 - PRIVATE PROPERTY

WL-1 PLOT 3.0 A. U.D

FOOD PLOT

CULTIVATED FIELD 9.A.

FOOD PLOT

RELOCATED U.S. RT. 33

7. 192 A. R/W

3.05 A.

OAK HICKORY

3.21 A.

OAK HICKORY

1.50 A.

-THE WOODS-
NATURE RESERVE
AND
TREE FARM
20.0 A
OAK-HICKORY
& OTHER HARDWOOD

November, 1983

The Director of The Ohio Department of Natural Resources (ODNR) sent the following message:

> *"We are in receipt of your recent letter regarding the relocation of U.S. Rt. 33 through your land. While we sympathize with your situation, there is nothing the Department of Natural Resources can do in terms of causing a change."*

November 9, 1983

This letter was received from the Administrative Assistant for Special Projects in the Democratic governor's office. It denied that a promise was ever made to meet with us as printed in the Columbus Dispatch newspaper (purportedly owned by a family supportive of Republican politics).

> *"First I must inform you that at no time has the governor promised to meet with The Rockenbaughs or accepted an invitation to visit 'The Woods.' The Columbus Dispatch is not the Delphi Oracle and has been known to misquote or distort reported events.*
>
> *Second, the plans to proceed with the highway project are designed to be in the greatest public good. Granted that John Rockenbaugh has worked hard to provide a natural sanctuary for plant and animal life, but it is his natural sanctuary and not the general public's."*

November 14, 1983

We received this stirring letter from Ohio Senator Howard Metzenbaum, or rather his staff:

> *"I am mindful of your concern about the proposed routing of this highway across your family's farm. I indicated your concern about the proposed routes to ODOT officials, and asked to be kept informed of all future developments."*

November 15, 1983

From the headquarters of The Nature Conservancy in Arlington, Virginia came these words:

"By copy of this letter, I'm notifying our Ohio Field Office director about your problem in trying to save The Woods Nature Reserve. If there is anything he or his staff can do, I'm sure they will be in touch."

November 16, 1983

The Assistant Director for ODOT sent the following summary of proposals that I had sent them. They elected to keep their proposal.

"Some pluses and some minuses are contained in your suggestions. Considering the advantages and disadvantages of your proposal, we have come to the conclusion to retain the alignment as proposed."

November 17, 1983

Received a letter from The National Wildlife Federation in Washington, D.C. with the following information:

"In regards to the highway relocation issue discussed in your recent letter, I can only express the Federation's sympathy with your concern and understanding of your feelings. However, NWF is limited by staff, time, and fiscal resources in becoming involved in the multiplicity of state and local environmental issues."

November 22, 1983

From Washington, D.C., The American Forestry Association wrote:

"From our standpoint, yours is a localized cause which, though certainly meriting support, is best understood and supported by state forestry or natural-resources group."

November 23, 1983

The Central Midwest Regional Office of The National Audubon Society in Michigan City, Indiana responded by letter with the following:

"I deeply admire your strong commitment to save the small natural area that has apparently been in your family for many years. It takes heartfelt commitment and dedication to do what you are doing to protect The Woods Nature Reserve.

You are following the only path available to citizens groups and individual activists; you are standing up to the pressure and for your own values. A meeting with the governor is as good as anyone can hope for, but keep the pressure on ODOT. Remember that it wasn't Governor Celeste who made the promise to Honda/USA, it was former Governor Rhodes.

Your experience is but one more example of how shortsighted economic decisions can play a negative role in both quality environment and ecological preservation.

Please accept my regrets that we can't be of more assistance to you. Keep the pressure on. Inform and involve as many voters as you possibly can and get commitments from elected officials. ODOT answers to them.

From what I can see, you are doing a great job!"

November 30, 1983

Wrote to The Ohio Forestry Association seeking their help. Receipt of my sincere letter of desperation was never acknowledged.

November 30, 1983

The following story summary appeared in The Columbus Citizen-Journal:

"State transportation officials have proposed that a new, expanded 17 mile stretch of U.S. Route 33 west of Marysville run about 1,000 feet south of the existing section of Route 33.

State officials also said that the route provided the easiest access to the Honda of America plant."

Officials used the promise of an expanded Route 33 to lure Honda into the area in 1979. Objections from a community group that claimed that widening the existing section of Route 33 was too dangerous prompted the proposal of 4 alternative routes."

December, 1983

The Sunday Columbus Dispatch featured a story that included the following breaking news, purportedly involving ODOT's District 6 Deputy Director:

> *"The Ohio Department of Transportation is investigating reports that one of its employees planted state-owned trees at the suburban home of a department official."*

(The home of ODOT District 6 Deputy Director, who earlier wrote that I had: "taken a posture lower than the animals I was seeking to save.")

December 9, 1983

A welcomed letter was received from The Ohio Field Office of The Nature Conservancy, in Columbus, Ohio, stating in part:

> *"We understand the love you have for your woods and the satisfaction you receive from your stewardship of it.*
>
> *We have been in touch with the Administrative Assistant for Special Projects in Governor Celeste's Office and with The Ohio Department of Transportation.*
>
> *ODOT was very impressed with the depth of concern for seeing The Woods protected and indicated that the Department was very willing to work with you in every way possible to lessen the impact the rerouting would have on The Woods.*
>
> *I think you will receive shortly a letter from the Department of Transportation with some very positive suggestions."*

December 10, 1983

Great news came the following day from the Administrative Assistant to the ODOT Director:

> *"As Assistant to the Director, I am familiar with the numerous letters written by you and others concerning The Woods. A stage has been reached in this exchange of letters where it seems more damage is being done than good, more anger expressed than ideas and more distrust created than understanding.*
>
> *I believe you are sincere in your desire to preserve The Woods and the wildlife it supports.*

I believe you want your children to grow up to appreciate this natural setting.

The highway being planned will have a negative impact on your Mother's property. However, the Department has said that it would make every effort consistent with a safe and workable design, to reduce the impact this roadway will have on The Woods.

Although the highway will not go around the utility tower as you desire, the alignment has been moved much closer than indicated on your diagram.

The major portion of The Woods will be intact."

And so, 133 days after seeing a broad pink band representing a new highway through The Woods and the farm were to be destroyed by another special-interest highway plan, The Woods were spared.

On Tuesday evening, January 10, 1984, WBNS 10TV came to our home in Richwood to do the third, and happy-ending, news story.

The final tease prior to the 11:00 PM News that night opened with Reporter Mike Horwitz standing in front of our home:

"Inside these four walls a family takes on the State of Ohio and says: We've won!

...I'm Mike Horwitz and I'll tell you their story next... on Eyewitness News."

Dave Kaylor, co-anchoring Eyewitness News at 11:00:

"And good evening everyone. Here's what's happening tonight at 11:00."

Lou Forrest, co-anchoring Eyewitness News at 11:00:

"The news is still sinking in tonight—the promise of more jobs and a better economic climate in Ohio, because Honda of America is expanding its Marysville Operations. Ohio offered a lot to Honda, tax incentives and an expanded state route were among those promises. Well the promise to make Route 33 bigger and better is starting to come together, but that turned into a nightmare for at least one family."

As Mike Horwitz reports tonight, that family took on The State of Ohio and won its battle!

Reporter:

When John Rockenbaugh first saw the Department of Transportation's plans, he was flabbergasted! No matter what, the State was going to push Route 33 through family property... property The Rockenbaughs call: 'The Woods,' a nature reserve they've worked 10 years to groom and maintain.

The State said, 'progress is progress!' The Rockenbaughs said. 'Nothing doing!'

So they and friends started writing letters... lots of them."

Scene from the desk of Assistant ODOT Director's office stacked with letters and him talking about the flood of letters:

One from Marion, three from Massillon, one from Florida, one from...

Reporter:

ODOT admits, without this slew of letters, they would have forged ahead!

Assistant ODOT Director:

We would have likely... uh... followed along on the path we first set.

Reporter:

But that didn't happen and the plans were redrawn!

ODOT Bureau of Environmental Services Administrator pointing to the new plans and explaining:

We move from...from a point up in here, further south to the point we now take approximately 4 acres.

Scene returns to our living room with reporter:

Yeah! We can live with that for sure! I said.

Reporter:

"That's exactly what John Rockenbaugh and his family wanted... to preserve the nature they have allowed to flourish." Their campaign with ODOT seemed almost compulsive at times... and discouraging."

"... Sigh... it was tough! It was a rollercoaster ride that... uh... emotionally left you down more than up!" I said.

Reporter:

"And so Highway 33 will be expanded and rerouted to accommodate Honda and the extra traffic.

ODOT is speeding-up the design and engineering phases of the project and expects to start construction in early 1986.

33 will go through some homes and through some properties and the people will be compensated. But it won't go through the major portion of The Woods... for which The Rockenbaughs say: 'There is no compensation!'

—Mike Horwitz, Eyewitness News... near Marysville."

January, 1984

A week later we received a tardy, though typical, response from The Clark County (Ohio) affiliate of The National Audubon Society stating:

> *"I am sorry for the delay in answering your letter but due to the holiday season, we have not held a board meeting until this month.*
>
> *At our January Clark County Audubon Society board meeting your letter was discussed.*
>
> *As property owners ourselves, we are most sympathetic to your problem.*
>
> *However, we decided that because the property is private and without significant natural uniqueness, it is not within the C.C.S.A. organizational mandate to become involved on either side of the discussion concerning the highway through your property."*

Thanks, but no thanks!

One of the most disturbing aspects of this battle was our state representative's suggestion that we hold out for their best offer and go buy land elsewhere.

I was stunned.

How could I leave this most-special place on Earth? It was here that I saw my first whitetail up close. It was here that I discovered the yellow-shafted flicker and sweet scent of goldenrod. The farm was home to the magenta-colored thistles that doubled as a source of nest down for the late nesting American goldfinch. The farm was always a place that I looked forward to going and hated to leave. The Woods is where I walked beneath the full moon and felt the color of pastel blue upon my skin. It was within the woods that I heard the soft sound of snow falling and the baritone hoot of the horned owl.

In April, The Woods grew ankle-deep spring beauties. By October I was waist-high in wood asters along its borders. It was here that I effortlessly climbed trees to look out upon June fencerows waving in tall ripe fescue and Timothy. So have my young sons. The farm is where dad introduced me to a sweet patch of wild strawberries whose progeny remain today.

I discovered the seasons in great detail while walking the fields and woods. Winds here were windier and the fresh air more intense.

I learned a great deal about colorful sunsets at the farm.

God inspired me to do something special with these woods.

I was not about to be chased-off by an errant highway. I would not surrender to a plan devised to fulfill promises to a foreign-based company that was lured and enticed to locate here by a lame-duck governor.

How could she even begin to suggest that we hold out for big bucks and buy another woods somewhere else?

Draft Environmental Impact Statement, 1984

The battle was over, or so I thought. The 200 pages of correspondence to date proved to be just a mere beginning.

The Draft Environmental Impact Statement (EIS) was being prepared for circulation on or before January 16, 1984. I had 30 days to review and comment upon its findings. Close-out date for comments would be March 19, 1984.

Environmental Impact Statements (EIS) are written to satisfy the law and benefit the preparer as necessary. They remain great works of facts and greater works of half-truths.

Its opening statement read:

> *"The proposed project will construct a multi-lane, limited access freeway on new location to relocate and improve approximately 17.0 miles of U.S. 33 between U.S. 33—C.R. 28 intersection in Logan County and the U.S. 33, U.S. 36, and S. R. 4 interchange with the Marysville Bypass in Union County.*
>
> *The Project will require the acquisition of 736 acres, including 100 acres of wooded area and 471 acres of prime farmland, and will take 7.68 acres of wetlands. Seven (7) streams will be affected. The project will also displace 20 residences and 2 businesses."*

If that were not environmentally-insensitive enough, much more environmental neglect would follow.

The Draft statement says that:

> *"Much of the natural vegetation in the project area has been cleared for agricultural purposes, and only isolated woodlots remain interspersed among cropland, pasture, and fallow fields in various stages of succession."*

One would think, and perhaps wrongly believe, that these remnants are unworthy of further protection. After all, succession would just lead to bigger and better woodlots.

ODOT admits that:

> *"Three properties in the project corridor are subject to some wildlife management."*

> *One is a young 28 acre woodlot composed of second growth hickories and oaks with some white ashes located on the Rockenbaugh property and considered a nature preserve by the owner. This woodlot lacks a defined understory, and its sparse ground cover consists of Virginia creeper, white avens, various grasses, poison ivy, and other species. Management activities have been limited to the creation of several trails through the woodlot. No other wildlife manipulation has been implemented. This property is not open to the public."*

The statement failed to recognize the 250-year-old white oak that measured 13 feet in circumference. It did not mention the many 150-year-old -plus swamp white oaks that tower over the "young 28 acre woodlot." It did not mention that black walnut and black ash grows there. Sizeable red, pin, and swamp white oak grow there too. It did not mention the wild black cherries, honeylocusts, crabapples, and hawthornes. Hackberry and elm have homes there too.

The statement did not recognize the very well defined understory and dense ground cover that included: spring beauties, fire pinks, wild geranium, golden ragwort, woodland sunflowers, blue phlox, wood asters, goldenrod, turks-cap lillies, rue anemone, jack-in-the-pulpits, green dragons, wood anemone, purple cress, obedient plant, pennyroyal, yellow hawkweed, yarrow, gray beardtongue, oxeye daisies, deptford pinks, blue-eyed grass, Mayapples, violets, heal-all, cut-leafed toothwort, trout lillies, pussy toes, Greek valerian, fleabanes, fringed loosestrife, jewelweed, New England asters, and more.

To have found all of these, ODOT scouts would had to have spent a year, not just a few hours in early spring doing an inventory. What was important to ODOT was making sure the highway plans would not be imperiled by announcing that common white avens and poison ivy were part of this "young woodlot."

Patronizing the Draft Environmental Impact Statement, ODOT added:

> *"Destruction of habitat caused by construction adversely affects terrestrial wildlife. Populations are displaced, and increased competition for food, cover, and breeding territory further reduces their numbers, especially in areas which are already at carrying capacity. Loss of wooded habitat means fewer species and numbers of terrestrial wildlife."*

ODOT must have read this less-than-profound summary somewhere.
The statement continues with more revelations.

> *"The project will affect a total of 278 acres of woodlands and successional habitat. In general, the loss of this habitat will reduce the overall abundance of terrestrial wildlife in the area. Most of the habitat consists of successional communities or second growth oak-hickory woodlots which are relatively common throughout the project corridor."*

Soon the common and fragmented woodlots will be less common.
The statement assured us:

> *"The Project will not require land from any existing or planned public park or recreation area, or wildlife and waterfowl refuge."*

ODOT remains preoccupied with public area concerns, while refusing to acknowledge that our nature reserve is a wildlife refuge of its own.

The Draft EIS for this project is a beautiful piece of environmental fiction.

Comments were solicited from highway friendly agencies. My comments were sent too.

Final Environmental Impact Statement, 1985

"It is anticipated that the Notice of availability for this document will be published in the Federal Register on January 18, 1985. The review period will expire on February 19, 1985.

There was nothing new and different with the wordy Final EIS version.
Those commenting on The Draft EIS included:

Ohio Department of Administrative Services, Division of Public Works
Ohio Department of Health
Ohio Board of Regents
John Rockenbaugh
U.S. Department of Housing and Urban Development
Valley Hi Commission
Ohio Historic Preservation Office
Paris Township Trustees
U.S. Department of Commerce, National Oceanic and Atmospheric Administration
U.S. Environmental Protection Agency
U.S. Department of Interior, Office of Environmental Project Review
Ohio Department of Natural Resources, Office of Outdoor Recreational Services
U.S. Department of Transportation, Office of the Secretary of Transportation

Most of the comments were politically-correct and kissy-faced. They were nauseating in nature to read. All had uncommonly and successfully played it safe.

My seven pages of comments concerning the Draft EIS were received and dismissed with simply: "Comment Noted." in ODOT's response column.

I actively participated in an environmental impact statement and learned how utterly worthless they really are. ODOT had said all of the right things to satisfy the law and to enhance the preparers' objective.

Again, I question how wildlife biologists could work for an agency that destroys wildlife habitat. It seems to me to be an act of chosen-profession treason.

There was one letter of support for our efforts from The United States Department of the Interior—Office of Environmental Project Review.

Their March 21, 1984 comment to the Draft EIS said in part:

"The U.S. Fish and Wildlife Service (FWS) advises that wetland creation must be an integral part of this project to be environmentally acceptable. Fish and Wildlife Service reiterates the comment made in its December 16, 1983 letter that utilization of borrow areas provide an ideal opportunity to achieve this objective. Fish and Wildlife Service has received a January 29 letter from Mr. & Mrs. John Rockenbaugh expressing interest in having wetlands created on their property to complement their nature reserve. This generous offer, including the possibility of using some of the area as a borrow site, should be investigated. For assistance in coordinating with Mr. & Mrs. Rockenbaugh, please contact the Supervisor, Columbus Field Office, U.S. Fish and Wildlife Service (ES), 3990 East Broad Street, Columbus, Ohio 43215 (telephone: FIS 943-6923 or commercial 614/469-6923)."

ODOT's response to the Department of the Interior's comment:

"ODOT does not presently acquire borrow areas. Individual contractors obtain these by contract with private landowners. ODOT has advised the Rockenbaughs of this policy and how they may contract for use of their property as a borrow site."

I had learned a lot from the experiences of the past nightmarish 18 months. I would learn much more in 1985.

I continued near-daily letter writing over the coming months. My objectives now were to get a narrowed right of way through our property; a pond constructed in exchange for free fill; trees left in the right of way; a 60" chain-link fence; wildflowers planted in the right of way; and wildlife cover grass mixtures.

All of government, and all its agencies, will never be free of the massive debt they personally owe me for impacting our private land that is dedicated to the Nature within.

Detail-less Design

Much of 1985 was spent asking questions about the details of the highway design. ODOT grew increasingly agitated with my constant written questions. Experience had shown that I must keep the questions coming—and coming often.

Perhaps the ODOT Assistant Director's letter of August 23, 1985 expressed their frustration best with the following:

> *"This will acknowledge receipt of your letter dated August 10, 1985 to Director Smith as well as your letters to me dated June 19, 1985 and July 24, 1985 concerning the referenced project as it affects your mother's property west of Marysville.*
>
> *It is unfortunate that our responses to your correspondence do not conform to your ideas of scheduling however, we do have approximately 2000 other programmed highway projects that do demand a considerable portion of our time. We submit that the records will show that we have been most generous with the time that has been devoted to this one element of the U.S. Route No. 33 project.*
>
> *With respect to the specific elements of your letters we offer the following:*
>
> *1. The right-of-way to be acquired through your mother's farm will be no wider that is necessary to construct and maintain the roadway section established for this highway.*
>
> *2. A chain-link fence 60 inches high will be provided along the highway right-of-way adjacent to The Woods. However, we will make no commitments with respects to color.*
>
> *3. The highway will be "blended" with the surrounding terrain through the wooded area, insofar as it is practicable to do so with a minimal right-of-way. This will be accomplished by using gentle back slopes on the ditch and preserving as many trees as is reasonably possible between the thirty foot safety zone and the right of way fence. If additional landscaping is found to be appropriate it will be done by separate contract after the highway contractor has completed his work.*
>
> *4. The standard ODOT wildlife seeding mixture will be provided between the highway ditch and the right-of-way fence through the area of your mother's farm.*

5. Deer crossing signs will be erected at the request of the Ohio Department of Natural Resources if their studies support the need for such signs.

6. ODOT does not participate in the creation of wetlands on private property. In previous correspondence we advised you how you may accomplish this through direct contact with the construction industry. We can and will advise you when this project is scheduled for bids so that you may contact prospective bidders.

The above commitments will be honored and the necessary elements will be incorporated in the detail plans at the appropriate time to be determined by ODOT."

The commitments were made to "my mother's property" west of Marysville. The fact that trees would remain in the right-of-way was unheard of until now. A week later The Wall Street Journal published a story headlined:

"Ohio Town gives look at Future for site of GM's New Saturn Plant."

It was a story about commerce, economy, greed, and progress. The lengthy article told how the Mayor of Marysville figured that 92% of the people were happy with Honda's presence. Honda, of course, justified its presence here just as Japan had justified its Sunday morning sneak attack on Pearl Harbor forty-three and one half years earlier.

The story concluded with the last paragraph and final sentence reading and undoing all that was glorified in the story:

"Down the road from Honda lives (we do not live there) Mr. Rockenbaugh on 22 acres of oak-hickory, which he has developed into a miniature wildlife reserve. The planned highway will cut off a corner of The Woods.

'I'm bitter,' he says. He plans to post a sign by the trail closest to the highway. It will read: 'Progress in America?'"

(Un)Fair Market Value

The project was moving towards the real estate appraisal segment to determine the paper worth of the 7.15 acres to be taken and to the 7.92 acres of landlock.

On Friday October 25, 1985 a licensed real estate appraiser from a distant county contacted mom to arrange a time on Monday October 28, to "appraise" the property. The time was from 1:00 to 1:30 PM.

Try to imagine a private real estate appraiser, contracted by ODOT, giving a fair and impartial appraisal. Try to imagine an appraisal that is anything more than a "windshield appraisal."

The Webster's New World Dictionary, Copyrighted 1980, defines real-estate as:

"1. Land, including the buildings, or improvements on it and its natural asset..."

On Monday October 28, 1985 we met with the appraiser at the farm. The vast majority of the time spent concerned the building structures, which are but fixtures placed upon the land for a deliberate use at some point in history. The buildings were a quarter-mile distant of the proposed highway and The Woods.

The Land remains.

We had to beg the appraiser to go back to The Woods. He re-stated, over and over again, that he did not want to "be led."

In the short time that the area was under appraisal he could not have seen the effective wildlife borders or the functional wildlife brush piles that were designed and constructed by our family.

He did not see the 12-box Eastern Bluebird Trail, and because of the late-date, did not see the blue beauty of this special songbird on the comeback.

It is doubtful that the appraisal included the many squirrel den boxes that were built and erected by our family to provide a higher standard of living for these woodland characters.

A walk along the earthen trails would have led the appraiser past the home of the flying squirrel who appropriated a den box.

Not far away was the summer home of the yellow-shafted flicker.

A tour of the trails would have placed one beneath the outstretched limbs of the old white oak and all of the history of its humble 1740 beginnings.

By appraising the area in late fall, one could not include the golden-yellow beauty of the hickories' leaves. By now, all of the colors have faded from the beauty of wildflowers that God had placed in them in previous months.

Late October is not a time of accurate appraisal in Nature. Perhaps it was not coincidental that this appraisal was scheduled for now.

We tried to get ODOT to have the area appraised in its summer fullness. Letters to ODOT dated April 13th, May 3rd, June 2nd, and June 19th seeking this appraisal request went unacknowledged.

If The Woods Nature Reserve, and the natural heritage that it represents, is not of greater value than brick and drywall buildings, then we as a civilization have truly missed the real meaning of life.

We have grown accustomed to the apathy that many display concerning the things of Nature. Attempts to enlighten unreceptive minds, such as his, are exercises in futility.

The appraisal was a joke as far as I was concerned. A windshield appraisal would have sufficed. The natural features of this land didn't matter to the appraiser.

At no time did I feel that non-income features were ever considered. I do not feel that proximity damages were ever weighed. I know that loss and enjoyment of the land was never understood. Damages to the remainder didn't seem to matter.

Was he familiar with this and similar properties? Was he familiar with local values? I think not!

All of these components are supposed to be an integral part of any condemnation appraisal. Nor did I ever see the highly specialized components that a condemnation appraisal is supposed to contain.

A condemnation appraisal is supposed to be definite, accurate, detailed, well-documented, well-researched, sound, and realistic. I saw none of these.

I distanced myself from the ODOT property agents ("closers") and their negotiations with mom… the owner of the property. I didn't like these characters and had no interest in their monetary values/interests of The Woods and farm. At this point, expecting the property agents, dressed in three-piece-suits, to understand the intrinsic value of this property would be senseless.

After several negotiations between mom, my brother, and ODOT, the property agent talked mom into signing the agreement on New Year's Eve 1985.

Mom is a very nice person from the Quiet Generation. A generation that did not ask for, look for, or find trouble.

I hear a different drummer.

The Conscientious Clearcut

One of my agreements with ODOT was to allow me to remove the trees in the defined right of way. While less than 3 acres of woods would be removed, it would be a neat and clean removal. There would not be damages to trees outside of the right-of-way.

ODOT(dom) said that I had until May 1, 1986 to have all "vegetative growth" removed from their right-of-way.

The following are from journal entries I made during the Conscientious Clearcut.

Saturday December 21, 1985

It was clear and cold when I walked alone to the highway area of The Woods and listened to the silence.

The cardinals made their appearance and the nuthatches worked the upper limbs of the swamp white oaks.

From 12:30 to 2:30 pm I cleared three to four hundred feet of old fence from the west side of the old abandoned road 141. This was preparation for the clearing that would soon take place.

Friday December 27, 1985

It was partly cloudy, windy and cold. I worked from noon to 4:30 pm. I surveyed the right-of-way and work limits for the intended highway. I was not alone. A red-tail hawk did his aerial survey from sixty feet above The Woods. Our work was not related.

Friday December 27, 1985

I went back to The Woods that night from 10:00 to 11:30 pm with my son Brodie just to walk. It was one of those perfect nights that included a full moon, snow-covered landscape, and the clear and cold associated with a high pressure system. We walked and searched the area for three-wheelers that violated the trails and non-trails of The Woods. Unknown persons enjoyed the trails from sometime after 4:30 pm until we arrived at 10:00 pm. It was my hope to walk the trails, second only to the animals.

Saturday December 28, 1985

I surveyed more right-of-way and work limits this day. My work began at noon and ended at 5:00 pm. I blocked the opening that was allowing trespassing three-wheelers to enter and exit with rolled-up old fence. They got my message later that afternoon.

While surveying I watched a large cottontail trot out of the neighbor's portion of abandoned road into our west woods. I stood quiet—motionless—as he came within 30 feet me… only to sense some fear while picking-up speed. As he continued on, two shotgun blasts resounded from a mile away. The rabbit stopped, then followed his tracks back.

I am glad that this healthy rabbit recognizes the sound of the "sportsman's." I am very glad indeed.

I watched what I assumed to be a jet stream in action. A narrow band of vapor-like clouds travelled across the clear sky from west to east at high speed. At very high speed.

Monday December 30, 1985

I again measured more right-of-way at The Woods and farm. It was very cold.

Tuesday December 31, 1985

I measured more right-of-way in the continuing cold from noon to 2:30 pm. I talked to my brother, Ron, about logs, and watched as a skein of geese flew south of the farm—heading southwest.

Thursday January 2, 1986

I went to The Woods from 2:00 to 4:30 pm. It was cold as I worked the right side to centerline survey in the west woods. I cut some hawthorns, small hickories, and elms west of the old abandoned road.

Saturday January 4, 1986

I returned to The Woods and farm at noon with my son, Cale, to work. Cale discovered some rocks clothed in moss. We had fun. I cut many hawthorns at centerline area 388.00.00 and 389.00.00 from 2:00 to 5:30 pm. I was very tired!

Saturday January 11, 1986

I went to The Woods at 8:30 am and stayed until 5:49 pm. I watched juncos, and sparrows flitting about the hawthorn cuttings. They stopped and flew to more familiar cover at the sound of distant blue jay squawks.

Sunday January 12, 1986

Worked from 2:39 to 5:49 pm. It was cloudy, cold and windy.
Returned home to celebrate my wife's 34th Birthday.

Saturday January 18, 1986

I went to The Woods to work the "Conscientious Clearcut."
(The highway right-of-way) It was cloudy and rather warm for January's winter period. It was a day of dullness—too wet to drive the car back. Working the pesky hawthorns seems never-ending.

I broke my trusty bow saw. It has been my working companion since December 1973. Perhaps I will repair it. I am certain that it has cut at least 5,000 trees to further benefit Nature. The saw has been with me through it all. It remains a very true friend.

Saturday January 25, 1986

It was a raw day in The Woods. Only the fat fox squirrels that crossed the old abandoned road brought me smiles. I saw at least four fox squirrels. They found safe cover, even though I posed no threats to them. One went into the brush pile at the "No-33 Trail" entrance. The others found refuge in the large old white oak at the entrance of The Woods.

Certainly we have realized success and reward by manipulating habitat to favor wildlife. Those who visit and travel the old earthen roadbed, comment on the abundance of fat fox squirrels seen at The Woods.

Today I began anew the "Conscientious Clearcut." I borrowed my brother's chainsaw and brought down about 100 pole hickories. I snuffed out their vertical life in the dormancy of their cycle. I am sorry.

An occasional tear tried to flow from my eyes, but I blinked them back in; such a lost feeling of despair to end the innocent and beautiful life of a struggling pole hickory. It isn't fair and it isn't right!

ODOT's property agent never understood this feeling, nor do any of the rest of the ODOT"s circus.

Nature is but an obstacle to ODOT's blind progress. They understand short-term economics, employment, and commerce. That is all. Oh yes, and political gain.

It is not unlike murder to bring down a quiet and unresisting pillar of life. It is cold-blooded murder.

Saturday February 1, 1986

This day started out partly cloudy in the morning. By afternoon it had warmed to 55 degrees with light rain.

The clearcut continued this morning. My son, Cale, and I were guests of the area, now technically owned by The State. Whether God intended it or not, I appreciated the warmer weather I was afforded for most of the day. The dismantled area of The Woods is most unnatural. There is too much light and too few trees. It has a rag-tag appearance.

It was not necessary for me to blink-back tears today, for I had too much work to do.

I must take stock in the fact that my conscientious clearcut is removing God-given vertical life to sustain wildlife in the fallen trees' horizontal position.

I began brush pile #2 today. It is a better brush pile in that it is sturdier and has condominium-style compartments. The hickory poles, 5"- 8" in diameter, and 18'-19' in length (heavy), were placed in the typical square log cabin arrangement. But this one has cross beams intersecting the mid-point of each side giving much needed strength and 4 private compartments. It is my hope that this hickory brush pile will be of greater value than the trees standing.

Saturday February 8, 1986

I returned this morning at 9:00 am to a temperature of 30 F., with snow flurries.

My presence was mostly ignored as I traveled the re-frozen earthen roadbed. The old road had begun to regain the posture it assumes in winter. A week earlier, rain had deluged the area. In a little while the old road will revert to its muddy state and remain that way through March. Travel will be impeded and work in the conscientious clearcut will be reached by foot, or by tractor. It is anticipated that this will be the last winter for the road without gravel. This spring should see a graveled roadbed.

Prior to my work in the clearcut, I make it a point to walk the area with a large cup of hot coffee. I re-introduce myself to the past and future devastation.

As I leaned against a firm young hickory, I heard the approach of a pair of Canada geese from the southwest. They flew forty feet above The Woods and me. Hinking and honking, they continued on—uninterrupted. I have noticed these two for quite a while. More than friends, they must be lovers. Lovers for life!

Two large hickory trees, with cling hickory nut husks, remain at station 392.50 LT. These trees will come down later.

I have tried to justify the killing of these trees by convincing myself that the individual neat death of each hickory is better than the mass killings by bulldozers; bulldozers that stack whole trees into piles and burn them to ashes.

In my conscientious clearcut, each tree will continue to live-on after death by serving as a wildlife brush pile, or wildlife borders.

I will not abuse God's wonderful gift to Mankind… a living tree.

Many, at least forty trees, have gone into a functional brush pile on the north side of the right-of-way in The Woods. The trees, in their death, shall continue to sustain life by being a source of safe cover, the foundation of a brush pile.

Many trees have lost their life in this area to make way for the highway for Honda.

I noticed that a nearby clearcut done by "loggers" at the Goodman woods left the land ravaged. The standing trees were splintered in the felling process.

Ours is a conscientious clearcut and all of the cuttings will benefit Nature, wildlife, and us. We are committed to that.

I cannot prove it, but I feel that geese fly over The Woods because it is predictably safe passage.

I seemed to make little progress in the clearcut… but I am not certain.

I am not where I want to be with my progress. I fear that I will not get the area cleared by May 1st, 1986.

Work continued on the brush pile, while the trees' fallen tops continue to multiply too fast to handle.

A heavy snow squall passed through, dusting the fresh cut stumps with a 1/2" of fluffy cover. I again listened to the sound of snow falling and wondered if I will ever hear such tranquility again?

Highways are too noisy!

Today, God allowed me to see the two geese. I heard the rascal calls of distant blue jays and listened intently to snow falling upon the logs of brush pile #2.

Thank you God!

Saturday February 15, 1986

It was a sunny to partly sunny day that was cold and breezy. Cale and I drove the Golden Jubilee tractor back to the clearcut. It was a day for Cale to learn the basics of tractor driving. The night before I purchased a heavy 16' long log chain for $32.00. It was money well spent, for the logs are getting too heavy to drag by hand. The faithful tractor, chain, and brute strength carried us up to darkness. We had skidded many swamp white oak logs down the old road and into The Oaks clearing.

I am learning the different scents of sawn wood as I work. Each species' lignin has a different aroma. Hickory, at times, has the scent of black pepper. I have caught its scent when burning, or cutting the tree. The aroma is not always present, but is very sharp when it is released. Ash has its own scent that I will refrain from attempting to describe, but will none the less always remember. White oak has a scent that is sweet and strong. It conjures-up memories of forestry shows and firewood splitting. To me, nothing can compare to the scent and memories associated with fresh sawn white oak.

I hate highways!

There is a loud popping noise emitted from oak as it leaves its sentinel post and falls hard to the frozen and snow-covered woodland floor.

There is a definite gap in The Woods Nature Reserve. The heavens are exposed. The clearcut is growing.

Saturday February 22, 1986

It was cold, cloudy, and foggy when I arrived at The Woods at 8:10 am.

I had to continue cutting trees that I do not want to cut and remove. Today was a day of cutting many 6"-8" diameter hickories in very muddy conditions.

Teresa brought Brodie, Cale, and T.J. down to The Woods with some delicious and hot potato soup she had just made. I love Teresa so much.

The boys stayed with me for the rest of the day.

I cut down a 6" diameter white ash and saw the beauty of its heartwood. Just as in people, the beauty of the heart is not readily seen in a tree either. Too often it takes an earthly death to discover the beauty of the heart. Indeed what remains are fond memories of a beautiful heart.

Sunday February 23, 1986

Brodie and I went to The Woods at 5:00 pm to pile the many tops of trees onto the wildlife brush pile.

Friday February 28, 1986

I took off of work today to go to the clearcut at 10:00 am. It was a sunny, but cold day. I finished skidding logs to The Oaks clearing and sawed some more oak. A cardinal could be heard attempting a full spring song, yet the chill kept it from perfection. The new log chain was very cold to the touch as I strangled and unstrangled each fallen tree with it. The aroma of fresh sawn oak failed to cheer me.

I hate highways and "progress"!

There was much work completed this day.

Saturday March 1, 1986

It was very sunny, but only 5 deg. F., when I arrived at the clearcut around 8:00 am. I faithfully returned to the "conscientious clearcut" to continue my self-appointed responsibility.

It was not a day of so much conscientiousness. Two friends came to help by cutting down trees for firewood. They are good people, who have good families.

It is my desire to help them out.

I assigned work in the triangle-shaped area farthest to the south of The Woods. They cut long and hard. The trees surrendered to them as they did me. Their killing was less sensitive and less personal.

I noticed my second robin of the new year. It was seen patiently shopping the softening logging path of the clearcut. I wish there was something I could do to make its task easier. Hunger is not a pleasant feeling.

The increasing angle of the sun seems to encourage the flow of sap in hickory stumps. I took a finger across the oozing stump and marveled at the sap's sweetness.

Again, the cardinals of The Woods sang. Better than yesterday, but still imperfect.

The day ended cloudy and I was very tired. Next week will be more conscientious.

Saturday March 8, 1986

I returned to the clearcut to slice a distance between The Woods' south right-of-way and the southeast centerline at station 393.00.00.

For just a little while, my brother Ron came to help me. He was amazed of how much work had been completed. My confidence restored, I skidded more logs to The Oaks clearing.

Ron began sawing small logs for another wildlife brush pile in the west woods. He seemed thrilled to help and be a part of building another heavy duty brush pile.

I plan to return next week… by the grace of God!

Saturday March 15, 1986

It was cloudy with temperatures in the 50's this morning. I finished placing bluebird boxes #4 and #5 into position.

As I cleaned-out the tiny sticks of a former wren nest, I noticed a single bluebird feather within, such a beautiful piece of brilliant art. The blue is ever-changing. In every light a different color of blue appears and disappears.

My brother came to help place the remaining tree tops upon the wildlife brush pile. The pile is all but finished.

A flu-bug sapped all of my strength. Little was accomplished that day as my brother left to return home to California.

It saddens me that I didn't get more done today. I was just too weak.

Ron will be missed until his return… soon I hope. I need his help. He is a good brother and a friend.

Saturday March 22 to Saturday April 12, 1986

Over 65 hours of labor attempting to finish the conscientious clearcut. I was too busy and tired to record journal entries.

Saturday April 5, 1986

A friend of our service forester came from Urbana, Ohio today to cut the large old swamp white oaks. Five of these trees line either side of the old abandoned road where the new highway will cross. All of the trees were over 115 years-old; one 30" dbh. (diameter at breast height), was over 130 years old. In less than an hour, 700 years of combined growth lay prone upon the soft litter of the woodland floor, the very litter that these friendly giants created. It is fitting that they came to rest upon the land that they made better.

Saturday April 19, 1986

Only the trees in the south fencerow remain. Our conscientious clearcut is nearly finished. Depression consumed me for the better part of the pm.

Earlier in the day I felled a 12" diameter white oak. I knew by the telltale sign of half-eaten nuts at its base, that the heartwood was hollow. I sawed into the tree about 17" up from the ground and watched as it fell quickly from the stump. In the hollow heartwood was a frantic mother deer mouse. She was nursing naked young and helplessly sinking into the fresh wood chips that blocked her exit at the base. I quickly cut a larger wood round from another oak and placed it upon the stump's top to form a heavy roof.

This is precisely the type of habitat destruction that happens with $tupid highways!

Out loud, I cursed the Ohio Department of Transportation, Honda, Japan, and all government officials! I am so bitter. I hate politicians, Honda, highways, and ODOT!

Sunday April 20, 1986

The absence of regular journal entries after March 15, 1986 in no way reflects an absence of effort or hard work. God seemed to have allowed me good weather every weekend.

The past month saw the most effort and cooperation to date. The days for me are long—13 hours! If it were not for Teresa coming down to visit and help, I would be much more tired and lonely.

The wildflowers began making their appearance in early April. Woodland cress, honeybees, and wood ticks arrived at the same time.

My work was done.

Friday May 30, 1986

Caleb, my 9 year-old son, writing in script, entered the following poem in my journal. I did not discover it for several months.

> *"May 30, 1986*
>
> *Birds*
>
> *Flying high, high,*
> *High in the sky*
>
> *Red, Blue, yellow, Brown*
> *Flying all over town*
>
> *Up, down, all around*
> *Making all kind of chirping sounds*
>
> *In the shrubs—one, two, three*
> *I saw one way up in a tree.*
>
> *Caleb"*

It was a precious poem, beautifully easing the pain associated with performing a conscientious clearcut.

ODOT's May 1st, 1986 deadline for having all of the "vegetative growth" removed from the right-of-way came and went. Succession began that very spring. The clearcut area became a mass of orange-flowered jewelweeds. Where they came from, or how long they waited for the chance of sunlight, remains a mystery to me. The suppressed pennyroyal, now ankle-deep, was also in abundance. By September, ten southbound ruby-throated hummingbirds were working the jewelweeds' amidst resprouting oak and hickory.

Tuesday March 10, 1987

The year's first pair of Eastern bluebirds was seen near a wildlife brush pile next to the conscientious clearcut. They were so pretty, as are any and all signs of spring after a long winter.

Monday March 23, 1987

At 8:40 am. I watched from a distance as a giant yellow bulldozer thrashed awkwardly in the 1.72 acre conscientious clearcut. It fed upon leftover tree stumps, but thrived upon earthbound roots. It was the first time that the monster equipment had made its way into the former woods. My heart and spirit sank!

Monday March 23, 1987

Unrest led me back to The Woods at 1:20 pm. this warm and sunny afternoon. ODOT and a contractor's associate were carefully measuring from the right-of-way stakes to the ditch limits. They were preserving the trees within the limits. Apparently the promise to save the trees was being kept by ODOT. As I watched them measure, the starved bulldozer continued to tear away at the innocent woodland floor, an area that had been preserved for years longer than my life and my dad's.

Monday March 23, 1987

A combination of curiosity and pain beckoned me to The Woods at 5:10 pm that evening. The bulldozer had crossed the old abandoned roadbed and stumbled into the west woods.

Such destruction.

An adjacent property's new borrow pit was still a center of activity at this late hour.

Tuesday March 24, 1987

I went to The Woods to see devastation. The dozer had gathered and shoved the stumps, complete with roots, into a burning pile that was slowly reducing them to ashes. Smoke moved with authority from the southeast to the northwest. The age-old stumps and roots glowed orange-white.

As the heap continued to burn, the noisy dozer, with a shining blade on the front and a large finger-like hook on its tail, wandered here and there. It reminded me of an overfed dinosaur seeking a place to sleep-off a heavy meal.

The gap in The Woods and the farm is bigger than life.

Life in The Woods will never-ever be the same.

The conscientious clearcut, though void of trees, remained a natural link between the two thriving woodlands.

As of this writing, there is no sign of life in the clearcut area, only upturned clay soil, fragments of dried roots, and redundant bulldozer tracks.

Thus, one woodland became two woodlands; two woodlands that add up to less than one.

The Conscientious Clearcut achieved its objective. Living trees on either side were not damaged. Wildlife continues to utilize the trees that were removed and made into brush piles. The hummingbirds of 1986 found migration fuel in the sweet nectar of jewelweeds that sprang-up in the clearcut. Over 60 sizeable swamp white oaks were skidded to the Oaks clearing and placed upon a drying rack.

These oaks would dry to serve yet another special purpose in our family's life.

Fresh Pond Water, 1987

Water was about to come to the farm from two different directions. One was invited, the other was not.

Our efforts to have a pond (borrow pit) built were successful due in great part to C. Clark Street, Executive Vice President of The Ohio Contractors Association. Mr. Street informed us who the prime contractors would be and who to contact within. I met with any estimators at the farm on my lunch hours. Our deal was quite simple and straightforward. Build the pond to our design and all of the fill dirt is yours for free. Most estimators figured that they would need around 90,000 cubic yards. This resulted in a 4 acre pond whose water depth would range from 8 feet to 24 feet in depth.

During construction of the pond I asked the project manager to please save all the large rocks that they found. He said they wouldn't find any. In a couple of days the glacial erratics appeared. Of particular interest was a complete Devonian Period Concretion. This spherical rock was born 360 million years ago. There were large pieces of granite and limestone found in the excavation that took all summer to complete.

When I asked the gentle bulldozer operator to save the rocks that were assembled in a pile on the pond's dry floor, he smiled and gave me a sideward glance. That night they were out of the pond area and atop the ground. He had never been asked to save rocks before.

The pond was successfully built next to the old abandoned road—west of The Woods. The contractor seeded the area with bromegrass, ryegrass, and fescue. We now had a large body of water to complement the woodlands.

Wildlife now has another place to grow.

Dirty Drainage Water

It wasn't long after seeing my copy of ODOT's detailed plans through the farm, that I found a serious error in their North right-of-way drainage plan. As proposed, the plans called for draining water from the highway and diverting water from a neighbor's field—directly onto our property.

Water had never flowed this way before and was inconsistent with the Final Environmental Impact Statement concerning drainage.

I wrote to ODOT of the design error. They sent a large topographic map that depicted the elevation contour lines. Using colored pencils, I clearly proved the drainage error.

It didn't matter.

I asked the ODNR Division of Soil & Water Conservation to meet me at the site of the former swale. Their report concluded that drainage had not flowed this way previously.

My appeals to ODOT, the Ohio Attorney General, and the Federal Highway Administration got nowhere.

My charges of "non-compliance" to the FEIS offended them.

They belittled me for not stating my exact concern, even though I had.

Their game of denial worked.

I wrote to The President's Council on Environmental Quality who referred it back to the Federal Highway Administration, who in turn found for ODOT's design as approved.

It was all a big joke to them.

The plans were already approved and the costs to change them would increase the project's price. Their bald-faced deception and cunning lies had worked.

My valid charges of "non-compliance" in regards to the FEIS drainage plans were ignored by ODOT, FHWA, the President's Council on Environmental Quality, and elected-officialdom. Everyone that I had sought assistance from chose instead to play it safe!

The error that I had identified in great detail was proven in less than one year. Today the ditch, unable to flow uphill to our land, flows nowhere. It contains stagnant highway runoff and diverted drainage that must seem confused.

Lush cattails thrive in ODOT's north right-of-way.

Their plans were wrong, as were the agencies that refused to help.

I alone was right.

In September, once the ditch dries-out, yellow government tractors mow the cattails down.

All is now ready for renewed growth and spring peepers come spring.

My Living Land Ethic—1987

It is my desire to share with others the land ethic to which I subscribe.

I am qualified to discuss ethics involving the land and the things of Nature, for I have experienced both the beauty of the land and the very forces that continue to destroy it. I know the indescribable miracles of spring, as well as the greatest enemy of the land—highway government.

Political promises were eagerly fulfilled to construct yet another land-consuming highway for private enterprise. It is repeated over and over again.

An ethic is but a single element in a collection of ethics that work together in an essential quality. It results in conformity to moral standards and proper conduct. An ethic is capable of making the distinction between right and wrong—based upon principles—rather than laws and customs.

The living conscience of moral principles is found in ethics.

One need not travel far into the country, or Nature, to witness the unethical abuses and neglect that civilization has placed upon the natural world.

Neglect of the land is continual. There are no new horizons of unethical conduct towards the land, only an apathetic re-run of past mistakes. To what end? An ecological dead-end.

When I refer to the land, I refer to every living aspect of the world around, above, and below us. The land is all of the things of Nature in one. It has demonstrated a remarkable ability to roll with the sucker-punches of so-called "progress," albeit, blind progress.

The land is forgiving for a while.

The Living Soil

The fundamental basis of life on Earth is in the living soil.

It is truly the seedbed of life itself, but to an insensitive highway department it is known as dirt, or fill.

A handful of living soil will sprout any viable seed. It takes millions of cubic yards of dirt for highway construction.

God only knows that enough living soil has been sacrificed for the endless miles of redundant highways that are built to serve some money-making enterprise.

Soil is more intangible, than tangible.

Living soil is as diverse as the plants it incubates and the Nature it sustains.

Soil is versatile to the living end that it serves.

Soil is sandy and soil is clayey… soil is ever changing.

I have seen the soil in disobedient dust devils and at the swollen mouth of eroded gullies. I hate erosion and will try to eliminate all that I see and don't see. Because I am not qualified to write about the technical science of living soil, I won't.

Deep in my heart, I feel that the living soil is something less because of our unnecessary reliance upon pesticides. What toxins are produced by the blending of these chemicals over the years?

Why are we so obsessed with the total eradication of every living thing in every field except the hybrid crops of government price support?

Ecology cannot work within these terrible constraints.

I love the aroma of living soil as civilization cultivates fields and backyard gardens in April and May.

The grasses that I walk upon, the wildflowers that I adore, and the precious trees that I admire, are all rooted in the living soil.

I respect the unseen crayfish community that resides upon our farm's soggy soil. They work into, and out of, the saturated clay doing far more good than their ankle-high mud chimneys reveal.

The groundhog is welcome on our farm. They do more for the soil than me.

I regret that I have not been a better steward of the living soil, but change is in the wind. My four year campaign with the Ohio Department of Transportation has vaulted my consciousness to the level of realization that it is the individual, not elected government—not government at all, who is responsible for soil stewardship that protects and defends the cradle of life.

The living soil is alive! The land is alive!

Still Living Waters

In all, I know little of water, only that it is required for life on Earth.

As much as any natural resource, water is grossly taken for granted.

This fact I realized first-hand a few years back. We live in a small village that has fouled ground water resources. I am told that our community's wells contain ammonia, the only wells in Ohio that do.

The Ohio EPA knows that the water is ill, as do village leaders. But four years after the fact, our family of six is still hauling supposedly safer water from another community across the county for our drinking and cooking needs.

I have attended public meetings where leaders are confounded as to what to do. The EPA blames village leaders for not acting. Village leaders blame the lack of money for not correcting the unknown origins of the toxic water supply. Purportedly, in past years, a bulldozer was seen working directly on top of bedrock at the village's shallow landfill. A landfill, accused of receiving midnight dumpings, is within several hundred yards of the community's wells. This site would be a place to begin.

While avenues for correction were being explored, we were assured by village officials that the contaminates present in the water were at acceptable levels. Whatever the levels of acceptable polluted water are?

Drinking our water was a game of chance.

It is this sense of confused priorities that place natural resources at the bottom of lists.

No greater threat to our groundwater resources exists than apathy. If one cannot see, touch, or smell contaminants... they must not exist. Dead Wrong!

Clean and pure water is a miracle to behold, if found.

Certainly I cannot see the aquifers beneath our county's Silurian bedrock. I am confident that they were clean and fresh at one time. This was a hidden treasure thought endless and forever free and safe.

Today safe water is found on supermarket aisles in convenient 2.5 gallon containers. Whole industries are capitalizing on bottled water and water purification systems for the home. It is no longer free. As a civilization we have come to the point of buying water—thinking that it is normal to do so.

I see the many forms that water takes in its continual cycle of attempted renewal. I imagine it in the puffy clouds and feel it when it falls from dark and dense clouds. I watch water as it flows in streams and drifts in ponds and lakes. I see it as designer ice crystals upon my winter windshield and watch as dusty July soil absorbs it.

I drink water and I exploit water by using more than I really need. Be assured that I will never take water for granted again.

There is satisfaction in knowing that morning dew slowly migrates down long stems of tall grasses each morning, a soda straw for any passing form of terrestrial wildlife.

There is unexplained goodness in the refreshing sight of fog rising above the area's ponds in June and October.

I walk around the puddles on our farm knowing that this collected water will evaporate before the Nappanee and Paulding clay soils absorb it.

Water affords me little time for study. I look at it, I feel it, and I wish that I could carry some in my pockets for the dog days of August.

What is water?

What will it take, and how long will it take, before we even begin to stop the careless fouling of our finite water resources?

How many generations before safe water can once again flow from hidden aquifers so deep?

Government officialdom will not correct the cause and damage. To do so would risk making waves in a society predicated upon the greed associated with progress. All we can expect of government is for them to play it safe.

It is up to individuals who are sick and tired of hauling supposedly safer water, in worn-out plastic jugs, across the county in order to have something essential to drink.

Trees

An acorn is a nucleus of an ecological wonder to behold, but to never fully understand, as hard as we may try.

A single tree is but a forest in waiting.

It is of and for trees that I write a land ethic at all, I suppose.

I am at peace in The Woods and find it a chapel as well as a refuge from society and business enterprises. I am closest to God when in The Woods. The church that holds my membership cannot compare to the sanctuary I find in The Woods.

Trees influence my life beyond explanation, and in ways I am unable to communicate.

I yearn for the companionship of trees and find solace beneath their varied limbs and leaves.

There are many trees that I recognize and many that I do not. I find it unnecessary to know every sub-species, for I am just thankful that they elect to grow upon our cooperative land.

Perhaps the shagbark hickory is my closest friend in Nature. I seem to know it better than the rest, perhaps owing to the fact that 8 out of 10 trees in The Woods are hickory.

I know the oaks that two generations before me knew. They remain strong and beautiful on our farm… seemingly ignoring the aging process.

To admire trees is to appreciate God's grandest gift in Nature.

When I observe a forest, I do not see a source of lumber, or once-in-a-generation profits of a timber sale. I am convinced beyond doubt that the role of the forest is not fulfilled in squirrel stew, venison steaks, and railroad ties.

To observe a solitary tree, or an entire woodland, is to witness and behold a functional miracle that transcends generations.

A miracle of a tree begins in the living soil; is sustained by living waters; and ends in the living soil. The soil is made richer by the tree's presence—alive or dead.

A tree will never acknowledge our fondest thanks or sincerest appreciation. It is comforting to know that a tree does not live for recognition… only purpose. Civilization could take a lesson from the life and times of a tree.

What quality remains after a tree has served its visible purpose is known only to the biomass. Even in the death of a tree, it continues to support and make life possible for others. It may be a cozy first home for a newlywed pair of woodpeckers; a safe hideaway for a deer mouse; a pulpit for mushrooms; or just an ample supply of rich organic matter for the living soil.

A tree never lives or dies in vain!

Entire volumes could be written on the beautiful benefits of trees. I choose but a few lines to express my thoughts in knowing trees and regrets in not fully knowing trees.

I will attempt to explain my love for trees and fail. I accept the frustration of the dilemma as the way it must be.

There are coveted trees and so-called "junk," or "weed," trees. I reject this unfair discrimination—for I love all trees.

The fact that the robin builds her nest in the crotch of a hawthorn, or upon the needle-sharp clusters of a honeylocust tree, makes them not weed trees. They are special trees, with a purpose that increases the evolutionary success of other species in Nature.

Civilization seeks oak for furniture, hickory for heat, ash for tool handles, and cottonwood for short-cord filler. I seek them all because they are alive and serving me by their standing presence.

There are not too many trees, nor are there enough trees.

Trees are not obstacles of civilization, but rather the literal pillars of civilization.

Like other natural resources, trees are exploited for various reasons, usually for dollar profits; exploited to the extent that only because trees are miracles do they continue to exist at wall.

What person can ignore the functional beauty of a single tree in flower, leaf, or fruit; or turn from an autumn woodlands for something greater?

> *"Leaves teach us how to die. One wonders if the time will ever come when Man,*
> *with his boasted faith in immortality, will ever lie down as graceful or as ripe."*

Thoreau

Wildflowers

I make no distinction between wildflowers and flowering weeds because the bumblebees and honeybees do not.

There is a world of beauty in all wildflowers, both from a distance and particularly beneath a magnifying glass.

The dandelions attract as many honeybees as do the sweetest of clovers.

To me, spring beauties in early spring are as special as the fire pinks during the perfect days of June. Neither are any less than the sweet-scented plumes of September's goldenrods waving impatiently at southbound monarch butterflies.

In November, when visible life on the land is waning, a few renegade asters hang-on to announce the winter. The bright red clusters of jack-in-the-pulpit fruit offer contrast to the now gray and brown woods.

God is a master gardener, too!

There are countless wildflowers growing and thriving where they are best-suited. It may be a rocky field, a lush meadow, an ignored ditch, or among the reliable woodland leaf litter.

I have watched as the jewelweed entertains our four children with the catapulting seeds of the dangling pod's hair-trigger. I have watched the jewelweeds seduce a swarm of nectar-loving hummingbirds. There is approving wonder in the eyes of those who mince on the jewelweed's seeds for the first time and compare it to the taste of walnuts.

The tinkers weed has proven interesting simple because it is a tinker's weed.

While there are no dinosaurs in our woods, the green dragon's crimson fruit cluster becomes visible upon September's woodland floor.

My thoughts are that every adorned wildflower, and every so-called weed, has its own story to tell in due time. It has a functional role to play in the bigger-than-life ecosystem that it inhabits. Their challenge to us is to notice them.

It may not be obvious, it may make no sense at all, in fact, it may have no discernible connection whatsoever, but wildflowers play an important role in Nature. Their assigned niche is but an extension of their right to one seat and one vote in life.

My own convictions lead me to admire and co-exist with the entire wildflower community. I use no mechanical or chemical control to decrease their presence or numbers. Wildflowers are best tended by simple observation.

What a colorful gift we have in God's wildflowers and flowering weeds. What if we were to ask a blind-from-birth person, given ten seconds of clear sight, what they thought of a green field sprinkled with the dandelion weed in its robust yellow flower?

Grasses

Grasses!

Everywhere are grasses!

I have overlooked their importance for most of my life and discovered that they didn't mind at all.

Grasses have always served to make the landscape greener and have filled in the blanks between rocks, fence posts, and sidewalk cracks.

I have no extra favorite grass, for I am still a stranger to most. My dad introduced me to Timothy grass when I was young. Years later, I continue to look forward to walking and viewing Timothy fields. They seem to endlessly wave like a great green flag in an all-day breeze.

I am most familiar with Timothy grass and like it because my dad did. Subliminally, it may have been the reason we named our youngest son, Timothy.

I enjoy the simple pleasure of walking through tall grasses for reasons I am unable to communicate.

I discovered that the bottle-brush grass finds our farm suitable for growing. Its value is unknown to me, but I admire the character of its namesake silhouette.

Teresa and I sowed a mix of Indian grass, big bluestem, and switchgrass in a small plot north of the great old white oak. We introduced our children to native grasses that once were part of the vast pre-settlement Darby Plains—just 15 miles south.

In my observations I have noticed that bluegrasses emerge first to reclaim the land from whatever its former toil. Of course it is done in good faith and never asks, or expects, any reward.

I know of no grass that offends me… period!

Grasses seem to cooperate as well as they can dominate. They are most tolerant, diverse, and forgiving.

Not unlike the impromptu wildflowers, grasses seem to grow and thrive where they are best suited. This makes our decisions easier.

I will not pretend to understand the valuable roles that grasses play in our ecosystem. I find it only important to know that grass is green and the world depends upon a certain quantity to sustain life.

I am satisfied that grasses grow because they are supposed to. They never seek my approval of their worth, or complain when I walk upon them.

Wildlife

Wildlife is the visible character and personality of the land.

Wildlife is more than rabbits, squirrels, and deer; it's songbirds, butterflies, snakes, bees and spiders.

Wildlife is wild… wildlife is life!

The greater the land is made capable, the greater the numbers and diversity of wildlife it will support.

To me, a minority, wildlife is not game.

Wildlife is the citizenship represented by a land ethic that respects the land as a free community of self-government, perhaps better defined as a passive anarchy.

The sport hunter and profit-minded conservationist view wildlife as a game. Their contribution is killing, or harvesting, wildlife. My contribution is providing habitat for wildlife to increase and diversify. I am for wildlife because so many are not.

We do not have too many deer, rabbits, or groundhogs. In fact I find great satisfaction in watching groundhogs and deer foraging at sunset.

As with all wildlife around The Woods Nature Reserve, they live out their lives without the threat of being conquered and displaced by human civilization. It is obvious that the family of deer walk our soft woodland trails as evidenced by the various-sized tracks left behind. I like that very much.

I love all wildlife. The mosquitos, which I involuntarily feed, are loved by dragonflies and bats.

All that I ask of the wildlife community is to mingle with them as they go about their business in the natural world. I come not to rule and conquer, but to watch and learn. Even the skunk is not my enemy. I fear him not from the safe distance I maintain. My observations have shown that the skunk wanders aimlessly in late winter. His entrance and exit into The Woods is wherever his nose is when it crosses the tangled borders of purple and brown black raspberry canes.

At night, my car's headlights are magically reflected back through the eyes of raccoons along the old abandoned road.

The wildlife on our farm know many thresholds in and out of The Woods. The Eastern bluebirds know one, while the blue jays know another. The white tails know many, while the cottontails know a proven select few. The butterflies and moths are not particular, nor are the walkingsticks and the nosey dragonflies.

I suppose that the tens-of-thousands of spiders could care less which door they use. All they must do is be in place in time for the feasts of August.

All of the passages of The Woods are safe refuge with no obligations. I am glad that all of the wildlife are present, for my purpose is to attract and sustain viable populations.

Wildlife imparts a special quality to the living land that cannot be fully measured by any given generation. To the extent possible, wildlife has proven to be adaptable to much of civilization's blind progress, albeit in reduced numbers.

We push wildlife around as though we own them. We don't. Civilization shoots them, traps them, cages them, and stuffs them.

What is it about the head of a beautiful buck in rack that drives humanity to nail it to painted plaster, or to a simulated oak paneled wall in a recreation room?

To me, it means that the deer was unable to outrun a merciless slug, or avoid a piercing arrow that was shot from a bush, by hunters that eat at least three meals a day.

Wildlife remain the greatest victims of progress in America. As they go, so shall we.

Unmendable Fences

My 1987 land ethic was an extension of my sincere feelings and imperfection.

An ODOT North right-of-way stake was found facing our property, at the boundary line, with the following admonishment: "Stay Clear, Assholes!!!" It was boldly written in indelible black ink. The long orange and yellow ribbons, streaming in the breeze, did not soften the profound statement.

I began to realize how far I had distanced myself from a government I once wrongly respected and never knew.

There were more mistakes to correct before the highway opened. One in particular involved the fencing contractor who was about to install the standard 47" woven wire right-of-way fence when I stopped them. I flagged down a passing ODOT official, who was going nowhere until 5:00 pm. He took me to the nearby ODOT field office to hear my case. There I found another bureaucrat with cataracts that would not hear my complaint. The next morning I called ODOT District 6 to talk to their boss. Calmly I read the chain-link fence specifications off of my set of plans to him. Once I gave him the project coordinates, he exclaimed, "You're right, you're absolutely right, John!" Later that day the fencing contractor began pulling the wooden fence posts out of the ground. They would return to place steel posts in cement for the 60 " chain-link fence that was negotiated and promised.

Before the proper chain-link fence was finally erected, a farmer, who had contracted farming rights on adjacent ODOT-owned landlocked farmland, cut through our west property tree line and fence to get his corn crop out. Ours was the only property without a fence. I confronted the farmer and asked who gave him permission to cut the fence, remove the young trees, and cross our property? He said: "ODOT!"

Calls to ODOT resulted in denial of ever having given the farmer permission.

Who was lying? Who cares? When would the comedy of errors ever end!

We dismissed the incident as just another dirty chapter in the Big Book of Progress!

Not So Grand Opening

On Thursday, September 1st, 1988, at 9:30 a.m., Relocated United States Route 33 was opened to traffic from Marysville to the Honda plants. The ribbon-cutting ceremony featured the Mayor of Marysville, a state senator, the state representative, who earlier suggested we go buy property somewhere else, the Union County Commissioners, the president of Japan's Honda/USA, and all disconnected forms and levels of autocratic ODOT.

Traffic, particularly semi-trucks, were whizzing by the farm and past the land that was once quiet, innocent, and private. Noise, visual distractions, and odors accompanied the cars and trucks. Litter soon followed.

We held our own docile protest rally next to the chain-link fence. It featured a large homemade sign that read: "RT. 33—DEAD END FOR NATURE." In addition, all of the trash that I collected before the highway opened was on display in our overloaded farm wagon, litter that was created by construction workers. Still in its place, on our side of the fence, was the ODOT survey stake reading: "Stay clear Assholes!!!"

Our quiet protest lasted all day. Reporters from the Columbus Dispatch and The Cleveland Plain Dealer dropped by to ask questions. Both did stories that were objective, but kinder to so-called progress than to Nature.

It was time to accept the fact that life at the farm, and within The Woods, would never be the same.

It was also a time to reflect upon the past 5 years of conflict and success.

Without a lawyer, our 2,000 pages of correspondence resulted in The Woods being preserved. The realigned route took the fewest acres of trees possible. The right-of-way was narrowed through our property and trees were left in the right-of-way. We had a 4 acre pond built at no charge and a 5 foot tall chain-link fence erected to keep in rabbits and keep out trespassers. A wildlife grass mixture was planted on either side of the highway, along with purple coneflowers.

Without a lawyer, we challenged the Final Environmental Impact Statement findings. From local agencies, clear to The President's Council on Environmental Quality, all were submissive to a drainage plan that was full of error. Although the errant drainage designs were never changed, our charge of non-compliance was proven the following spring. Cattails continue to grow where diverted drainage water fails to run uphill onto our farm.

Our experiences taught us so very much about the folly of representative government and the greedy egos that continue to contaminate it.

The Zip Code on the front of the U.S. Post Office in Marysville reads 43040. It does not, however, give any hint that this area is in reality a Japanese Occupied Territory.

We watched as the Empire of The Rising Sun changed the community forever.

We discovered that conservation organizations only want your dues, not your concerns.

We learned how shallow-in-character, both Republican and Democratic politicians really are. The only difference in the two is that, one is in office and the other wants to be. We learned how ineffective government agencies, even ones charged with protecting the environment, can be and how powerful the autocratic Ohio Department of Transportation is. Even though it is an agency riddled with design errors and inept political appointees.

There is no commitment to preserve our living environment. Government wrongly believes that its success is measured in the same cruel way that private enterprises are.

What I learned most of all is that politicians and government agencies survive, not by character and convictions, but by steadfastly playing it safe!

All of government, from this day forward, will never-ever be out of my debt.

Roadside Litter, 1987 – 1992

Litter, it occurs unnaturally throughout Ohio's towns, townships, and counties in ever-increasing amounts. Litter marks the boundaries of our highways and serves as a high-low water mark along our ditches, streams, and rivers. Litter is a mighty flotilla of ecological ignorance and apathy upon our lakes and ponds.

In an otherwise civilized society, litter, and littering, remain a persistent glitch. It has become a trademark of human intrusion and activity. Wherever civilization has been—litter remains.

The most visible by-product of "progress" is litter.

Even before the highway opened, litter was making its presence known on our farm, in The Woods, and in our newly constructed pond. Construction workers thought nothing of throwing out whatever was left after breakfast, lunch and breaks onto the right-of-way.

I choose to include this post highway opening episode to illustrate just how far government is out of touch with environmental concerns.

Having picked up thousands of pieces of litter from our property during construction of the new highway, I was shocked to see how much more there was after it opened.

On December 3rd, 1988, 3 months after relocated U.S. Rt. 33 opened, I wrote a kind letter to the ODOT District 6 Deputy Director. I was asking for a permit to collect roadside litter where the limited-access highway crossed our farm.

There was no response.

Keep in mind that this was already the third ODOT District 6 Deputy Director since 1983. It remains a very political appointment.

A brief follow-up letter was written on January 9th, 1989 to the deputy director. However, I decided to send Xerox copies of it to the following: The Governor, the ODOT Director, our Congressman, our State Representative, our U.S. Senator, the Ohio Department of Natural Resources Office of Litter Control, the Union County Office of Litter Control, The Top of Ohio Resource Conservation & Development Project, and the Union County Commissioners.

In a letter dated January 11, 1989, the deputy director stated that our request was denied.

At this point I wrote to The Governor asking his assistance in helping me secure a permit. In addition, I wrote another letter to the deputy director with Xerox copies again going to all of the above.

I received yet another denial of our request from the deputy director. It appeared that he was beginning to enjoy saying no.

Letters were pouring in from all of the officials and agencies I had Xeroxed copies to. They all said that there was little that they could do, but for me to keep trying.

I did… they didn't.

On February 6th, 1989, I received another denial of my request for a permit to collect litter from the deputy director.

His silly little game of denying me—not my sincere purpose, had gone far enough.

On February 11th., 1989, I wrote a lengthy letter to the Inspector General of The State of Ohio outlining the difficulty I was having in trying to obtain a permit to collect roadside litter from the highway through our farm.

On February 28th, 1989, I received my fourth letter of denial and the admonishment: "Any further correspondence regarding this matter will be futile."

On March 4th, 1989, I engaged in an act of civil disobedience, or rather obligatory civility, and went out onto the highway right-of-way to collect litter. I was wearing an orange vest and supplied my own litter bags. I collected over 800 pieces of litter from just one side of the right-of-way for one-half mile.

The litter included: 30 aluminum cans—mostly beer cans; 47 empty cigarette packages; 53 Styrofoam drinking cups; 25 wax coated drinking cups; 32 bilingual shipping labels; 1 black t-shirt; 43 plastic drinking lids; 6 cardboard boxes; 37 plastic and cellophane bags; 7 losing Ohio Lottery tickets; a diesel fuel filter; an oil filter; a mud flap; 3 old newspapers; many disposable cigarette lighters, and a lot more.

I sent the entire inventoried list to the deputy director that day.

On Tuesday March 21, 1989, the Inspector General's Office called me at work and sternly requested copies of all correspondence I had with ODOT to date.

They were not impressed with ODOT's unprofessional responses.

Out of the blue, on May 19, 1989, I received a cordial letter from the ODOT District 6 Deputy Director stating the ODOT Director had authorized offering me a permit to collect litter in a Pilot Program for Ohio.

My application was forwarded to ODOT. After many technical delays, we received a permit and legally collected the first roadside litter on November 10, 1989. It included the two mile stretch of U.S. Rt. 33 through the area of our farm.

The Inspector General's Office did not mess around. ODOT(dom) was now doing all it could to cooperate with us in the Adopt-A-Highway Litter Control Program.

I only wish the Office of Inspector General had been in place in 1983.

My reign of terror over the highwaymen ended with this event. I had seen enough careless mistakes to last a lifetime. I had to move on.

Billboard Blight, 1989

While litter was attempting to get through the chain-link fence, yet another nemesis associated with modern highways was about to destroy our tree-studded western vista.

On a sunny morning in April of 1989 I was driving past the farm on relocated U.S. Rt. 33. I did this on occasion to keep an eye on the property. As I approached the farm's west property tree line, I noticed a pick-up truck parked along the berm. In the same instant, I saw a large pin oak come crashing to the ground. Our 27.5 dbh pin oak was crashing upon our land. Someone was cutting trees from the south to the north along the property line of the north right of way. It took me ten minutes to get to a phone and call my brother at work. I told him to get his camera and meet me at the farm as soon as possible. In 15 minutes we were confronting the chain sawyer. My brother was taking pictures of everything, including the sawyers and their parked truck.

The young man was scared. He showed us crude penciled instruction on a yellow sheet of legal pad. It instructed to remove all trees in the fencerow for 80 feet. His work was being done for the wood in order that a billboard company could place a billboard on the neighbor's property.

The young man gave us more information than we needed, plus the crude instructions. He apologized over and over again. He stated that he had just recently found God and begged that we wouldn't hit him. Neither of us had even thought of physical force. Supposedly he was doing this work on his own in return for the firewood. There, on the ground, on our property, lay 12 sawed off trees that we owned. There were 2 red oaks, 1 white oak, 5 pin oaks, 2 elms, 1 hawthorn, and a shagbark hickory.

He was in a hurry to leave, but sheepishly asked if, when this was all over, he could have the wood? My brother and I exchanged quick glances and said, "No!" He understood.

What else could go wrong? Now we were staring at a 60 foot long gap in the tree line that we had worked so hard to preserve. The trees grew right up to the right-of-way fences. Now this.

An arborist came to the farm to review the destruction and write an estimate for damages. His estimate figured a loss that totaled $28,146.04.

My brother's attorney began proceedings in mom's name. The billboard company denied any formal connection with the young sawyer, except to give him the wood in exchange for cutting down the trees. Of course the billboard company denied instructing him to cut our trees. That is what I would say too, if I were the crooked billboard company. It came to light that billboard companies do this a lot in order to clear the way for their ugly advertisements. If they get caught, they apologize and settle. It is cheap in the long run to do business this way.

A long series of correspondence exchange took place over the next 8 months between lawyers and insurance companies. Quite frankly, I stayed clear of the lawyer jargon and lost interest in the whole stupid affair.

It was my understanding that mom did receive a settlement. All that I know is that it was enough to pay for the thousands of tree seedlings we planted for the Conservation Reserve Program that the farm was now enrolled in.

Seven years later the basal sprouts (coppice shoots) have shot-up and now block the blank billboard that faces our property. On down the road there are many, many more.

In Paris Township, many now call it Tokyo Township, it is O.K. to put up billboards as long as they conform to state law. After all, billboards promote business and politicians!

I will be as clear, concise, and correct as possible in my fair criticism of zoning regulations that allow obnoxious billboards to flourish.

Present-day Marysville is surrounded by billboard blight. A drive around the outside edge of Marysville will reveal the landscape catastrophes. Many are still in skeleton form desperately soliciting with a phone number… begging to be exploited!

"I am yours for a little while… and for a price!" they seem to say. "Just give me a call!"

Is this what is meant by growth and development in all of the pro-annexation arguments? Is this progress?

No! This is an embarrassing environmental disgrace.

It was inevitable, only a matter of time, until the lack of protective zoning regulations reared its ugly head in the form of insidious billboards across the rural character of Marysville.

What are the costs of lost vistas and living tree lines to this disgusting form of pandering?

Beautiful trees, considered expendable until extinct, are the most visible and truly innocent victims of billboard construction. Any and all nearby ecologically-functional trees are felled, or butchered, to provide a wide-angle view of advertising litter.

In a more enlightened society, don't billboards offend rather than enrich the intelligence of the public? Isn't a business reputation earned… not "sold"?

Will Marysville simply rubber-stamp the zoning permissiveness that has allowed billboards to grow unchecked; and in plantation form, at the edges of town?

Since the City of Marysville and the Paris Township Trustees pretend to enjoy a disciplined cooperation with regards to future annexation—perhaps uniform and restrictive zoning that prohibit billboards can be written? But, who has the final say in an occupied territory?

Rural landowners and residents cannot be written-off as obstacles in the way of so-called "progress." They cannot be treated as second-rate citizens. They have every right to retain the living style they enjoy right now. This includes the right-to-farm and the inalienable right to an uncluttered sunrise and sunset.

Billboard overkill is just the beginning. The obsession with "bigger & better" growth and development is out of control!

Ohio Tree Farm 2174, Est. 1983

Standing in The Woods with his clipboard, he shook his head one more time and mumbled, "There's too many hickories!" Our friend, Jim Bartlett, a service forester with the Ohio Department of Natural Resources' Division of Forestry, was perplexed.

In March of 1983 we met on-site to discuss a management plan that would benefit the trees and wildlife. It was obvious that The Woods needed work to release promising, though suppressed, hickories and oaks from stagnant competition. My personal walking stick, a strong hickory tree, displayed over 25 annular rings that fit perfectly in hand.

I did not know where to begin, but Jim did.

In November of 1983, with the highway's location still unresolved, Jim began marking trees for removal in a 5 acre plot. He asked more than once if I was certain that I wanted to do the timber stand improvement in this area. I told him that if the highway is not rerouted, ODOT would be responsible for destroying more of my efforts at natural resource stewardship. I was confident that ODOT would reroute the highway, or rather so hopeful that it mimicked confidence. A month later it was re-routed.

By the end of the day over 1,000 trees, mostly multiple-stemmed hickories, were splattered with blue paint dots. These stagnant trees, dead-end trees, would be removed to improve the health and viability of competing trees. Dead trees, "snags" as they are called, were left for wildlife use and humus building. I would have a busy winter.

All of the blue dotted-trees were felled during the winter's week-ends. All went into wildlife brush piles in log form. Their tops were added to the pile and along the edges. I do not recall cutting any tree over 8 inches in diameter. Most were 3 to 6 inches in diameter. Cutting the trees seemed endless. After a hard day of sawing, blue dots seemed to mock me. They were everywhere.

Slowly, I could begin to see the "crop" trees that were "released" from competition. By "crop" I do not mean a saw log, or future source of income, but rather a tree allowed to shoot up and expand its canopy and mast production.

One of the unexpected rewards discovered in the five acres of TSI came the following spring and summer in the form of wildflowers. From out of nowhere appeared a mass of red-hot Fire Pinks (Silene virginica) and cool Blue Phlox (Phlox divaricata). It was in the improved timberstand area that I saw my first Eastern bluebird on March 24, 1984.

My eldest son, Brodie, was with me when the beautiful male appeared along the woodland's south margin. He was nine years old, and I was 32, when we saw our first bluebird. It was a moment that

I will forever cherish. Our efforts reduced the timber basal area from 120 square feet to 80 square feet per acre, whatever that meant.

With 5 acres of timberstand improved, we decided to improve 5 more acres. The following winter we continued the clearing of stagnant hickories. An oak, any oak, was allowed and encouraged to stay by thinning-out its competing neighbors. Many more wildlife brush piles were created. This portion of the TSI project followed along the area that would have been the centerline of a new U. S. Rt. 33. I discovered that The Woods was home to the flying squirrel that lived in a honeylocust cavity. My youngest son, T.J., always wanted to go with me. It was at age two, that he watched me work in the TSI area. I remember one cold day as he watched attentively from the warm car's child seat—then dozed-off for a nap. Even in his naps he smiled. I stopped and walked to the car to watch him sleeping cozily through the windshield-such a miracle. I dropped to my knees and gave praise to God—through sobs of happiness. Once again wildflowers seem to leap out from beneath the forest litter as sunlight reached new areas; Wild geraniums covered an area where I had never seen them before.

On April 25, 1985, a few days after finishing the project, my wife gave birth to our beautiful daughter Tracie.

Four months later my daughter would look-up from her cozy position in my arms and smile in wonder at September's waving leaves at The Woods.

As a result of this timber stand improvement project, we were named Ohio Tree Farm #2174 by the American Tree Farm System.

The familiar green and white Tree Farm sign was presented to our family of six by our forester, Jim Bartlett. A picture was taken standing in front of the great old white oak.

I better understand the role that forest management can play in a given woods. It was remarkable to see how fast the released-from-competition trees responded with growth. Young white ash jumped to attention in the opened forest floor. The stratified understory was better defining itself.

It was my decision to do TSI on only 10 of the 20 acres of The Woods. A part of me wanted to retain the untamed woods that was determining its own order. This was the woods I found so many years earlier. In geologic time The Woods will determine what grows best where.

I do not agree with many of the editorial positions of The National Tree Farmer magazine. In fact, most tree farmers boast that the measure of a successful tree farm is in the number of stumps found. I don't get it. They do not understand the plight of endangered species or endangered wooded wetlands.

I became so disgusted with the on-going editorial position attacking wetlands landowner's rights, and the Endangered Species Act that I sent a mean-spirited letter directly to the editor and publisher. My fiery letter was sent directly back to the Ohio Tree Farm Committee with a recommendation to decertify our tree farm. The committee spoke to our service forester who explained our position in a lengthy letter. He wrote as one who understood. It opened eyes and minds heretofore closed to other possibilities. The TSI experience enabled me to see how trees could benefit from thinning.

Our Tree Farm is now more than just 10 acres of TSI. We have planted over 13,000 young seedlings to fulfill requirements of the Conservation Reserve Program. Fields that once reluctantly grew stunted soybeans and giant ragweed are now growing white ash, green ash, sweetgum, red oak, pin oak, swamp white oak, bur oak, Norway spruce, and sugar maple. In the meantime, natural succession is filling in the blanks with enthusiastic elms, and native oaks and ash.

Perhaps disproportionately, our farm is growing a lot of ash.

We planted a large amount of ash because it grows well upon our farm. More importantly, because, since 1959 when I became a New York Yankee fan for life at the age of seven, I have loved baseball and the crack of the bat. Oh, the sound of the homerun hardwood—ash!

Ours is a not-for-profit Tree Farm.

Ohio Tree Farm Sign Posted

On Oct. 29, the John Rockenbaugh family was awarded an official tree farm sign and certificate presented by the Ohio Department of Natural Resources' Division of Forestry and the Union County Agriculture Soil Conservation Service in recognition of their 10 acres of managed woodlands at The Woods Nature Reserve located on US 33 west of Marysville. The recognition earns them certification into The National Tree Farm System, a program beginning in 1941 to promote the wise and continual use of our woodlands. Rockenbaugh is only the fourth tree farmer in Union County to receive such a sign and certification. Pictured from left, Jim Bartlett from the Ohio Department of Natural Resources' Division of Forestry, Brodie, Caleb and Timothy Rockenbaugh, John and wife Teresa with Tracie.

An Oak Log Cabin, 1985 – 1991

During the forced Conscientious Clearcut of 1986, it became apparent that the swamp white oak (Quercus bicolor) was the dominant sizeable tree removed from the soon-to-be-impacted 3 acre area. Their age was around 65 years old. We concluded that the last timber harvest was in 1920. However, large swamp white oaks along the adjacent abandoned road were around 130 years old. Simple math deduced that the first timber harvested from the farm was in the 1850's. The old abandoned road was indeed surveyed in 1853. Perhaps it opened the area to a convenient timber harvest. Aside from the two 240 year-old low-crotched white oaks, trees undesirable to loggers, there are no trees older than 135 years-old on our farm.

The John Deere 1010 skidded the frosty logs down the winter-hardened earthen road to the clearing in The Woods.

There were at least 60 swamp white oak logs. Fifty had uniform size to be used in a log cabin construction. The oaks averaged 11 inches in diameter at the base to a useable 6 inch diameter 14 feet later. After that, taper quickly took its toll.

The logs were cut to 14.5 foot lengths then jockeyed with a cant hook to a drying rack made of honeylocust and hickory logs. This rack would become a sheltered haven for rabbits and deer mice.

First racked in 1986, the logs continued to dry for nearly a year. The 8 largest logs were peeled by hand with a draw knife. They would rest upon 9 large pieces of granite, gneiss, and limestone. These piers were hostages abandoned by the late-great Wisconsin Glacier 10,000 years ago. They were wrestled by tractor and chain from their half-buried locations around the farm and skidded to the cabin's site

On the muddy afternoon of New Year's Eve 1986, Brodie, Cale, and I coerced them into their position around the log cabin's perimeter. They would rest here, 7 feet apart on center, to support and distribute the tonnage associated with over 50 oak logs.

In January, the largest and straightest 4 logs created the base of the cabin. They were painstakingly notched to perch forever on the contours of the boulders. The next row of logs, and all subsequent rows, was simply quarter-end notched to receive the mating log's diameter. It was the simplest notch to utilize.

The full-log cabin would remain only two logs high for over a year. There were still too many events, associated with the highway activity, for me to attend to.

In the fall of 1988, the rest of the logs were peeled and organized on the rack by their size. Three incline logs were placed upon the low walls to the ground. A rope was tied in two places to the foundation log on each wall. The rope was then looped around the next prepared log and pulled from inside the cabin area to easily walk the log up the ramp and into position. Here it was notched to fit the bottom log precisely.

I wonder what it was like to notch softwood logs that are often depicted in old movies.

To end-notch seasoned oak is an exercise in stick-to-it-ness and constant begging of forgiveness from God for things better left unsaid.

My tools were simple and consisted of a 21" bow saw, a 2" wide chisel, a small hand sledgehammer, a rafter square, a drawknife, a bit & brace w/ 5/8" auger bit, and a yellow crayon.

Each new log's end was measured back to accept the width of the log below. A few inches of overhang was allowed to give character to the corners. The logs' ends were crosscut one-fourth of the way through at the top and bottom with the bow saw.

The ends were squared-up with the rafter square, then marked with a yellow crayon. Sharp blows into the yellow lines with the hammer and chisel would create a relief notch back to the saw depth. Never was it a perfect notch.

The draw knife was used to even-up the mating surface. Seldom did I do more than a couple of logs a day. My forearm would ache from the repeated blows necessary to dislodge the notch material. That unmanned area, the arc between my thumb and index finger, would be called many things when the cold hammer would miss the chisel's head. A head that grew smaller in diameter, and a hammer—heavier, as the day progressed.

Keeping the wall square and vertical did not require as much attention as I figured. By March of 1989 the 4 walls were 10 logs high.

Work slowed during the summer months. The heat and feeding of mosquitos was not enough of an incentive. By late fall of 1989 the gabled ends were finished and the rafter logs squared-up to accept the roof''s 3/4" 4' x 8' outdoor plywood panels.

It would be the summer of 1990 before we would place flashing, felt, and brown shingles upon the roof. The west-facing door opening was cut out and framed as well as the south and east facing window openings. All were framed with boards cut from the five 135 year-old swamp white oaks that once lined either side of the old abandoned road where the new highway crossed.

The entire fall of 1990 was dedicated to chinking the spaces between the logs. There was still no floor, windows, or a door. Hardware cloth was secured between the log gaps. One part of rich mortar was mixed with 3 parts of sand and water to create a smooth gray-white chinking material. The outside walls were done first from bottom to top. The inside walls were then chinked to form a very character-rich effect.

On New Year's Day, 1991, Brodie, Cale, Timothy, Tracie, Teresa, and me worked together to clean-up all of the thousands of pieces of oak notchings inside and outside of the cabin area.

The following weekend I found a gray screech owl roosting comfortably in the cabin. It found its way out through the east window opening.

It would soon be time to consider building a door to fit the sturdy frame and to install the two imperfect windows that were donated to us.

The west-facing door began as a piece of 1/2" plywood neatly filling the door opening. On either side of the plywood, 3/4" planed random width swamp white oak boards, homegrown, were secured. The door, now two inches thick was secured directly to the logs with heavy hinges.

The windows were installed and trimmed with rough-cut swamp white oak boards

A simple loft was constructed in the east half of the cabin.

There were plenty of floor joists that joined two large oak logs that crisscrossed in the center of the 12' x 12' cabin floor area. Their intersection was placed upon the centermost boulder of nine. Exterior plywood was nailed directly to the joists to form the subfloor. Random width rough-cut swamp white oak boards were nailed directly through the subfloor and into the joists.

The sawmill's blade left excellent radial marks in the boards. The oak floor had character and needed nothing else.

Teresa bought a very old "Warm Morning" stove for me as a perfect 20th wedding anniversary gift. Its life to date had been spent in Union County. It would go in the cabin and remain loyal to friends and visitors of this Union County oak log cabin.

The cabin became a warm and special place with the stove's first fire on November 23, 1991. The stove was adapting well to a diet of oak and hickory. Heretofore it had foundered on coal.

Thanksgiving Dinner was served and eaten in the cabin 5 days later. Teresa cooked the entire traditional meal at home, then took it 17 miles south to the cabin that morning. I arrived earlier to feed the stove and warm the cabin. The sweet scent of oak was omnipresent.

It was a perfect Thanksgiving!

The aroma of turkey, mashed potatoes, sage dressing, scalloped corn, green beans, dinner rolls, and cranberry jell complemented the bouquet of fresh brewed coffee upon the stovetop.

Our family of six enjoyed this Thanksgiving in the cabin to the point that it is now an annual tradition that will no doubt transcend generations.

Construction of the cabin was a family affair. Collectively, my family fulfilled my dream by allowing me to pursue it. They had faith that my vision had substance.

Visitors seem awed with this simple cabin. They sit upon an up-ended log round, or at the oak picnic table, and take the whole atmosphere in. They ask many questions, but mostly they slowly look around with a smile of wonderment.

The cabin is always a welcome sight to me. In the summer it is a place to cool down and to escape mosquitos and deer flies. In the winter it is a cozy-warm oasis as curls of hickory smoke drift heavenward from the stove pipe. In the spring and fall, it is a perfect place on Earth to be.

In case the tax assessor ever asks, I will tell them the truth! According to The Ohio Department of Transportation, these logs are officially referred to as: "vegetative growth."

The gospel truth is that the cabin is nothing more, or less, than an orderly pile of condemned logs.

Memory Tree donated in honor of John by the Robinson Families.

Hunting

"Boom… boom, boom… boom!"

The silence that follows the blasts of a hunter's shotgun is usually perfect and welcome.

On a bright and sunny November Saturday, I heard the sound of rabbit hunters nearby. Since I was thinning small hickories with my silent bow saw, I walked out of The Woods and onto the old abandoned road to make sure hunters would not be shooting towards The Woods and me.

Just as I began to walk south into the warm-on-my-face sun, a volley of booms erupted. An eerie noise followed. It sounded as though someone had hurled a heavy wet stick that was cartwheeling through the air. The undulating swishing and swooshing noise was increasing as I turned my head to triangulate the source. Suddenly it crashed into an oak with the sound of an axe—six feet to my left and head high. I could hear the sound of shattered bark falling onto the ground.

In another second, I realized how lucky I was! It was a privilege to have heard, and be able to recall, the sound of a tumbling slug whizzing by me.

Miracles still occur.

I chased down the trio, running past the fresh fluff of cottontail fur that across the abandoned road like tumbleweed. I remember telling them that I didn't want to ever see or hear them again. While the others apologized, one stood silent with a smirk on his face. I suppose he was the sportsman shooting rabbits with shotgun slugs.

There have been many other examples of hunters hunting on our land without permission. I have confronted many trespassing hunters, whole platoons at times, and asked them to leave.

Some complain that my dad would have let them hunt. I tell them that I realize that, and agree that my dad was a very kind man. However, I am not my dad.

Somehow, working as hard as I do to manage and manipulate wildlife habitat for diversity purposes, is not fulfilled by shooting them.

I have never met the so-called ethical sportsman and sportswoman. To me, they are mythical characters created to sell shotguns and hunting clothes.

My earliest recollection of hunting was as a 6 year-old with my dad. He took me to the weedy flood plain of Bokes Creek, near my grandmother's house, along Hopewell Road. One of dad's friends had a bird dog. I learned that it was the hunter's job to shoot ring-neck pheasants that the dog pointed to. Once shot, the dog would retrieve it.

It was a good hunt. Just as I had hoped, we didn't see, or kill, any pheasants.

I didn't get it then, I still do not today.

On another hunt, I remember dad pushing over a rotted tree along the woods and watching as an owl tried to wake-up and fly at the same time. I learned then that it was wrong to disturb dead trees. To this day I contend that dead trees are just as important, and inseparable in value, as live ones. The Woods do not differentiate the difference.

As a young teen I tried my hand at hunting with a .410 gauge shotgun. It is the only part of my life that I regret. I could never bring myself to shoot a squirrel. I found no satisfaction or purpose in the killing of the rabbits and quail I shot.

Once, bored with inactivity, I shot a November downy woodpecker at close range. The vivid memory of watching tiny pieces of soft down float slowly to the woodland floor remains. To this day, I am haunted by that experience. I leave all of the snags that will stand to assuage the guilt that will never leave.

It was though actual experiences that I reached my position on hunting. Hunting may be sport, but killing isn't. Wildlife is life, not game.

I have never shoved my non-hunting position down anyone's throat. Yet, I am amazed at how much criticism I receive for not being a hunter.

A friend of mine, who is a professional conservationist, asked me one morning why I was at work and not out hunting deer in gun season. I gave the usual response that I hunt with binoculars and get my daily limit through them. I told him I was a preservationist.

He told me that this was his first year to hunt and kill a deer with a gun. He proudly justified his actions by saying that deer would become diseased and keep the herd from growing. Soon, without the hunter, deer damage would be out of control. He stated that his actions kept a deer from being killed by a car, thus preventing damages to the car and increases to my insurance premiums.

He had convinced himself of his worth, but not me.

I have heard all of the important reasons and justifications for hunting over and over again. It must be a pre-requisite in order to get a hunting license. I wonder; if the great American tradition of hunting was not licensed, would hunters still be called "conservationist" by wildlife licensing agencies? Agencies that exist as a result of these fees-please, spare me the lecture, I understand the role of wildlife management.

The hunter says that they keep wildlife populations at a healthy level. I ask how they know if they are shooting a prize stud, or sterile dud, rabbit? They shut-up.

How did wildlife in America manage before Indian and European settlement?

I am now left to conclude that it was indeed the absence of hunters that caused the extinction of dinosaurs.

A One-Term Supervisor, 1990 – 1992

I never knew who placed my name in nomination to serve as an elected supervisor for the Union Soil & Water Conservation District (SWCD). Or why? Especially after what I learned.

Rumor had it that it was a statewide push to broaden and diversify the base of Ohio's 88 counties' representation. It may have been intended to include perspectives other than that of the heretofore agricultural one. Or so I was told.

The voluntary position was marketed as local "self-government." I was assured in writing that it wasn't just another agricultural committee. I could make a difference.

In 1989 I accepted the nomination and was elected by the landowners and land users of Union County to serve as a supervisor for the 3-year term commencing in January of 1990.

At the annual banquet, a boyhood and lifelong friend of my late father, reached across the table with big hands and a smile and shook mine. He said that my dad would be proud of me. I was profoundly touched.

I wasn't sure what a good supervisor was supposed to do, but I intended to do my best. I was a maverick—so to speak. I was the first supervisor that didn't own a pick-up truck, live in the country, or make a living from farming.

I was one of five supervisors, but never realized a 20% voice

I apparently lived-up to the other supervisor's expectations of being a so-called "environmentalist." Often in discussions, the supervisors, albeit good people and successful farmers, would refer to those attempting to make the natural world a better place, as "tree-huggers." Anyone who wasn't a farmer was a "tree-hugger." They would then cast a sideward glance at me and apologize with a foot-in-the-mouth grin.

As a supervisor I constructed over 130 Eastern bluebird boxes for the district to sell over the three years. My labor was free, the district purchased the lumber. When I determined that too many boxes were becoming hose sparrow hatcheries, I stopped building them. Bluebirding takes a lot of commitment. House sparrowing—none!

I encouraged the selling of native wildflower packets and prairie grasses along with the established annual tree packet sale program.

When I suggested the purchase of a tractor-pulled tree planter they giggled to themselves. After all, farmers had been battling trees since settlement.

When I mentioned selling switchgrass (Panicum vergatum), one alarmed supervisor hollered, "Oh, no!" He mistook it for the fall panicum (Panicum dichotomilflorum) that wound around his combine's reel and wallet.

Our family hosted two SWCD county-wide forestry field days, and a four-county forestry-plus field day, at The Woods.

I tried to attend every meeting in the county related to natural resource stewardship. I publicly and adamantly opposed the proposed location of a landfill in The Darby Watershed. The Darby Watershed is recognized by The Nature Conservancy as one of the twelve Last Great Places in The Western Hemisphere.

I was reprimanded for not first seeking the board's position. The same thing happened with my Letters to the Editors.

I didn't care what the board thought. I was, however, disappointed to discover that the board suffered from government's familiar malaise of playing-it-safe.

I came to realize that the infamous 3-Way Working Agreement among The Soil Conservation Service (now the Natural Resource Conservation Service), The Ohio Department of Natural Resources—Division of Soil & Water Conservation, and the Union Soil & Water Conservation District is a lopsided agreement. Essentially it says that the SCS and ODNR will call the shots and the District will be the cardboard placard.

I sat helplessly as a point-source water pollution violator got away with breaking the law by simply ignoring the deadlines imposed.

Each year, at the annual public planning meeting, successful and kind farmers would attend and complain about silted-over tile outlets. It seemed to them that the roadside ditches were getting shallower. Never mind that their fall plowed fields were turning the drifting snow in the ditches brown as they complained.

Here is the crux of the problem. Fall plowing eliminates chancy spring plowing problems. It means less work when the short planting season does arrive. Erosion does not recognize wise economic plans. It never has. If one fall plows up to the ditches, one reaps erosion. The opposite is also true. This complaint happened each year I was on the board.

I was appointed to fill a vacancy on the Ohio Federation of Soil & Water Conservation District's State Education Committee in 1991. I attended my first state meeting with enthusiasm. My suggestion of a topic involving our treasured trees was selected as the statewide theme for the annual high school essay contest in 1992.

Later in the day, on another subject, I was stunned to hear a fellow committeeman, disgustingly refer to wetlands as "mosquito holes" and "mud puddles." However, the committee was chaired by a state FFA Alumni officer and was understandable.

I was not re-appointed to the committee the next year. I was never told why.

I had already made my decision not to seek re-election to the Union Soil & Water Conservation District's Board of Supervisors anyway.

Repeatedly I was asked, "Why not?"

I wanted to tell the bald-face truth; that I could lead (and fail) by example, but not by committee. A play-it-safe board of five was excess baggage.

I never got used to meeting with the county commissioners to review the district's budget for the next year. After all the scrutinizing and questions, commissioners would say, off-the-record, that we should have asked for more money—we would have gotten it.

I could see that it was getting easier for others around me to spend other people's tax money. I wanted no part of this.

It was indeed an agricultural committee, regardless of the official description to the contrary. Soil and water conservation districts were established to help farmers control erosion with practices that prevented it. Fifty years later they still do not get it. In essence, soil and water conservation districts will allow you to practice conservation as long as it doesn't interfere with farming profits

I believed in term limits and desired to show that I did.

I didn't support Affirmative Action, the government's version of reversed discrimination, and never would. I was not going to swear another oath of office to uphold it and other skewed civil right rules.

My philosophy for hiring district employees was to hire the best qualified person.

I attended too many Area SWCD Meetings where the topics were Affirmative Action, Hiring Minorities, How to Prevent Sexual Harassment Lawsuits, and other pressing social issues.

It was rare to hear anything about soil and water conservation.

I fulfilled my publicly elected term as a supervisor for the Union Soil & Water Conservation District on December 31st, 1992. I never truly "supervised" anything. Supervisors are better described as rubber stampers to the wishes of the other players in the 3-Way Working Agreement.

Was I a "good supervisor"? Probably not. I didn't fit into the long-established traditions.

Did I do what was best for conservation? Yes!

Richwood, Tree City USA! 1989 – 1995

Richwood is a family tree that reaches far and wide from its corporation limits in northern Union County. Unlike the county's seat, the Occupied Territory of Marysville, Richwood has no mean ego it cannot afford, just a lot of nice people.

About the same time that I was beginning my term as a supervisor for the Union SWCD, I was asked by the mayor of Richwood to serve as a Charter member of The Richwood Tree Commission. A recently enacted ordinance, Ordinance 96.00 -The Tree Ordinance, was now in place. Mayor Adam Shuman remembered when Richwood was a village that lived-up to its namesake. It was time to replant Richwood's urban forest and become a Tree City USA.

I agreed to serve and became the secretary of the Richwood Tree Commission.

It wasn't long before I realized a fear I privately held. I did not believe that natural resource stewardship can be legislated, or "ordinanced-in." I was right.

An ambitious tree removal program began in Richwood to remove the over-mature trees in the tree lawns. Most were dangerous car-crushing, roof-crashing, people-hurting silver maples. Still, they were summer-shady trees. My phone began to ring. In my quiet life, I never had ever received so much heated criticism for anything I was ever involved with. Tree lawn trees are, by ordinance, the village's responsibility. To the people, they are only the village's if they fall down; otherwise they are "the property owner's."

This thought process bore itself out over and over again.

As volunteering tree commission members, whatever we did was criticized! If we removed dangerous trees, or replanted recommended trees, someone would complain! If we did nothing at all, we were wrong. Even the village administration questioned the work of the volunteer tree commission.

I resigned from the commission 10 months into my first term. I was convinced that tree stewardship could not be legislated. I had my own trees to take care of, but I continued as a volunteer to help the village plant trees.

A few years later I was repeatedly asked by members to rejoin The Richwood Tree Commission. I did and again served as secretary.

For a year, this time, I worked as hard as I knew how to make a positive difference with Richwood's urban forest. While our time was in-kind, funding to care for the village's trees was never enough, or always in question.

Wildcat Woods, 1993 – 1996

Wildcat Woods is two acres of succession woodland located behind the Claibourne-Richwood Elementary School in Richwood, Ohio. It was the most hostile land form that I had ever experienced in my life. It was a former village dump, when it was common to tailgate glass, wire, and all forms of junk into shallow graves. The area had been inactive since the late 1960's. Boxelder, mulberry and silver maple trees had reclaimed the area in the name of Nature.

It was now a pioneer woods, complete with black raspberry canes, wild violets, and colonies of Dame rockets.

One could not take a single step without the sound of crunching old glass underfoot. Old cables and wire acted as inconsiderate snares.

Along the borders, giant fencerow trees of white ash and pin oak, cast welcomed shade and dwarfed the struggling trees growing in a seedbed of glass and twisted steel.

Yet this unaltered woods was the best-case example of the power of ecological succession. A few school administrators saw it as a potential land lab. I saw the possibility and more.

The Union Soil & Water Conservation District wrote a county-wide grant application seeking funding from the Ohio EPA's Environmental Education Fund.

It was accepted and Wildcat Woods became a reality.

Each teacher had a vision of what a land lab should be, but no one took the lead. In a joint meeting with administrators, I offered my free services and a suggestion that a trail network must precede all work. It takes many hours to "see" where trails would best work. I spent much time in the preliminary siting of this parcel, using established trees as areas where the trail would pass by.

A large refuse dumpster was placed next to the swamp white oak entrance to Wildcat Woods. In the coming months it would be overfilled with junk to the point that a larger garbage truck had to be brought in to lift and dump the dumpster.

Over 143 tons of #617 stone w/dust, eight dump truck loads, was piled outside the land lab. I loaded, hauled, and spread the stone to create over 2,000 winding feet of trails throughout Wildcat Woods. Each of the 715 single-axle wheelbarrow loads weighed over 400 pounds. Some of the haul distances were over 600 feet away from the stone piles.

Most of the trails were 5 feet wide and at least 4 inches deep. The immediate trail area was carefully raked prior to spreading the stone to remove the big pieces of glass and metal. The years' of accumulated junk did not permit digging down to a solid base. None existed for at least 3 feet.

The stone and dust mixture was very groomable and packed exceptionally well. After several months, the surface was very firm.

I worked in Wildcat Woods on week-ends and during my Christmas-time vacation. When classes came to walk and study the land lab, their feet on the stone pathway sounded like buffalo. A local wood pallet recycler was called upon to donate 16 cubic yards of seasoned recycled wood pallet chips to place upon the top of the trails. The trails became quiet and soft. A more natural sight and sound was realized. The grant enabled the purchase of 80 cubic yards of recycled wood pallet chips. It took a while, but I finished spreading the chips to make Wildcat Woods an area with soft and quiet trails. I donated two bluebird houses and a screech owl box. Of course the screech owl box was quickly appropriated by resident gray squirrels.

I logged over 500 volunteer hours in creating Wildcat Woods. In that special time I witnessed the American toad, red-bellied woodpeckers, nuthatches, cardinals, robins, bluejays, Carolina wrens, song sparrows, crows, mourning doves, black-capped chicadees, brown creepers, cottontail rabbits, gray squirrels, white-tail deer, and ground hogs. The ground hog excavations, at the entrance of their underground dens, were piled full of pieces of glass. It is incredible that they chose to adapt to this harsh environment of endless broken glass and junk. Winter saw a sharp-shinned darting through Wildcat Woods and the snow covered trails revealed shrew tunnels.

There is a diversity of trees in this young woods. They include the aforementioned as well as black walnut, wild black cherry, hawthorn, crabapple, apple, white oak, hackberry, and a large sycamore that became a well-recognized landmark deep in the woods.

Native rocks were placed near selected trees and painted with the trees species name. Various other pieces of limestone and granite were painted upon to illustrate the land labs longitude and latitude coordinates. The altitude above sea level and Lake Erie were also identified in this manner.

By the time the trail network was finished, I had overlooked, or turned-the-cheek, to many acts of youthful vandalism, acts such as placing rocks in the middle of the soft finished trails and breaking bottles over them. The clean-up was painstakingly slow. Other acts included: discharging school bus #8's fire extinguisher in the middle of a soft trail; blazing trailside trees with a dull knife; scarring trees by beating upon them with big sticks; and pre-teenage smoking. Littering was excessive.

I turned-in the names of those responsible to the school, but it didn't do any good.
On the evening of Friday April, 19, 1996, my daughter came home from Wildcat Woods to tell me that all of the printed rocks had been dug up and overturned. Kids were down there breaking bottles as she told me.

I watched the youthful rodents, genetic clones of their parents, beating on trees and breaking bottles. When I confronted the two repeat offenders they told me that they were having "fun"!

I took my gloves off in order that I would have something in my hands other than them. I shook my head, unable to speak, and walked from Wildcat Woods to the chorus of the American toads.

My work was forever finished at Wildcat Woods.

Wildcat Woods will survive. In time, the teachers will learn ways to teach in this great outdoor classroom. I revealed many secrets to the students and teachers that visited Wildcat Woods. One secret that I found most promising was the hundreds of tiny pin oak seedlings that were growing ankle-high in the land lab. These oaks will one day dominate the land lab and cast welcome shade upon the former vandals in their old age and in the life and times of their great-grandchildren.

I was able visualize and realize the potential of Wildcat Woods. It will become the single-most important classroom that the students will ever learn from.

Arbor Day at The Richwood Lake Park

Teresa asked me to come along and help with Arbor Day 1989 at the park. The park board was going to assist the North Union's 5th graders in a clean-up of litter and planting of trees at The Richwood Lake Park. They were using the recently written Comprehensive Tree Planting Plan that was written exclusively for the park by the Ohio Department of Natural Resources—Divison of Forestry's Urban Forestry Section.

I was very impressed with the enthusiasm displayed by the students and teachers. Here were students planting trees to make the 13 acre park a better place.

The next year I was more deeply involved, and brought the Union Soil & Water Conservation District into the picture. They would donate white pine seedlings to each student and staff at the end of Arbor Day at the park.

By 1991 I was coordinating the event. I found natural resource professionals to present afternoon environmental education programs at the park's two shelter houses. The three North Union elementary schools, representing the area in and around rural Richwood, came together as one to plant trees and collect litter in the morning.

It became known as annual The NU Arbor Day at The Richwood Lake Park celebration.

Each year sizeable young trees were planted in locations specified on the plan.

The Richwood Lake Park was previously home to cottonwoods and silver maples. There were a few catalpas and a couple of Norway maples.

The plan called for over 90 new plantings. Each year the list grew shorter as the number of district students involved grew longer.

It took the cooperation of the North Union School Board, The Village of Richwood, The Richwood Tree Commission, private donations, The Union Soil & Water Conservation District, Blue Spruce Nursery, and the Ohio Department of Natural Resources—Division of Forestry and Division of Natural Areas & Preserves to fulfill the plan.

Each spring I would go to the park the week before Arbor Day to site and dig the pilot holes. This was necessary because the park was situated around a lake that was once a gravel pit. Much overburden was spread in the park area. In this spoil were many fist sized rocks that seemed to form caches. The obstructions would have prevented the students from easily digging in the allotted time. It had to use picks to pry apart the limestone nests.

Over the seven years I had pre-dug over 70 holes. Each hole took about 3 hours to properly dig and refill—less the rocks. In this way, each student was able to easily dig the hole, plant the tree, and refill the hole without the numerous and cumbersome rocks.

By 1995 the plan was nearing completion. The park now boasted diverse plantings of swamp white oak, red oak, bur oak, Kentucky coffee tree, white ash, sweetgum, Winter King hawthorn, baldcypress, European larch, crabapples, river birch, globe arborvitae, sea green junipers, golden rain tree, forsythia, burning bush, rose of Sharon, Austrian pine, amur maples, Japanese tree lilacs, Miss. Kim lilacs, serviceberries, Japanese kerria, and Aristocrat flowering pear.

Over the years others had planted trees in the park that didn't follow the plan, but were no less welcomed. They included Japanese red maple, Red Sunset maple, Norway Spruce, and various cultivars of crabapples.

By 1996, the official written plan was within sight of completion.

A series of events, revolving around the school district's voter's failure to pass a key spring levy, nearly kept two of the three schools from participating. A brilliant busing strategy, endorsed by the board, allowed all three schools to participate.

With an $800.00 donation from The Richwood Tree Commission, the final eight trees were purchased and planted on Arbor Day 1996.

It fulfilled the plan as written. Nearly 1,000 fifth graders and staff had collectively worked together for seven Arbor Days to transform northern Union County's only park into a beautiful park. My son, T.J., and daughter, Tracie, had been two of them. My job was eliminated too. There comes a time when new blood and enthusiasm is needed. That time was at hand. I faced increasingly more obstacles and frustrations in executing the celebration each year. If it were not for trees, and seeing the plan completed in detail, I would have turned it over to someone else.

When I now ask some now older student at the park which tree he, or she, planted they proudly walk to the exact tree and smile.

Something far greater than trees had been planted!

Volunteerism's Crash & Burn, 1979 – 1996

I unintentionally misplaced my life's compass in 1979.

Heretofore it had been a precious piece that unfailingly pointed to The Woods.

Others began to encourage me to help with this, and to help with that. It had always been my nature to do things without pay. I felt most comfortable doing things this way, for my parents had. Perhaps I could help others by volunteering my time. Maybe I could make a positive difference?

It innocently began by helping the Marysville FFA Alumni raise scholarship monies in honor of dad. Dad was a tireless supporter of FFA and had moved onto eternal life preparing to go work at the annual FFA appreciation breakfast in 1979.

His $100.00 check for Life Membership in the FFA Alumni Association did not clear prior to his death. In his honor, I sent in my own $100.00 to fulfill a desire he could not.

My role as a fundraiser escalated into my being President-elect of the Marysville FFA Alumni Association. I wasn't at the meeting that nominated and elected me. I asked that my name be removed as president for I wasn't interested. I think that they saw an opportunity for more fundraising. I wasn't the fundraiser, or president, they had hoped for.

In the early 1980's I was nominated to become a Deacon for The First Presbyterian Church at Marysville. I accepted what I thought was a high honor. I discovered that the role was that of carrying out the business and protocol of the church. My position was to assign ushers monthly for each of Sunday's two services, (only one in the summer), and be prepared to fill in for any that did not show. This went on for three years, 36 months.

I learned a lot about The Church Inc., too much to keep me coming back.

The highway ordeal vaulted me into the nomination and service as a supervisor for The Union Soil & Water Conservation District. While there I was the district's representative to the bureaucratic Top of Ohio Resource Conservation & Development Project. I served on the Ohio Federation of Soil & Water Conservation Districts' Envirothon Steering Committee and the State Education Committee. All of these required time I didn't have.

Events then snowballed. I became a trail monitor for Bluebird boxes along Rt. 23 in Delaware and Marion Counties. I became a bluebird and kestrel trail monitor for the Top of Ohio RC&D Project's boxes along relocated U. S. Rt. 33 west of the farm.

I served on the ODNR Division of Wildlife's 1990-1995 Strategic Plan representing songbirds, particularly bluebirds.

I wrongly thought that my example would encourage others to pick up the ball and run.

I began getting phone calls to conduct tours of The Woods from different organizations. I hosted an International Assembly of Mennonites for an afternoon outing at The Woods. I took off time from work to arrange tours for a hospital auxiliary, a creative pre-school, an Awana youth group, and more. My phone at work began to ring too much. Many well-intended people were demanding, not asking, of my finite time.

It was hard, no impossible, to say no! I had created a monster that I must somehow now slay.

I was nominated to serve three years on the Extension Advisory Committee for the Union County Office of the Ohio State University Extension program. I fulfilled that commitment representing Community & Natural Resources Development concerns.

Through it all, there were still the NU Arbor Day at The Richwood Lake Park, Wildcat Woods, and Forestry Field Days to properly attend to.

I did two years of a voluntary service as host and instructor with a teacher's in-service program called: "Acorns to Oaks" at The Woods. It was written by The Ohio State University Extension. The Union County 4-H Agent co-instructed the course on Central Ohio Teachers Association day in October of 1993 and 1994.

Still there was overwhelming work to do with The Richwood Tree Commission.

It was on a cold January night in 1995 that I violently hit the wall.

Volunteerism's granitic wall remains unscathed, though.

At its musty-smelling darkened base, where nothing germinates and cruel shadows hide, the weak pulsating glow of a few remaining embers are now extinguished.

Alone by myself, I survived the soul-jarring wreckage and the searing heat of the great Crash & Burn. It has been an extended recovery, but I can now clearly see the endless blue skies and feel the gloriously warm sunlight that the igneous monolith had insidiously been eclipsing for the past 17 years.

My collision, at wide-open-throttle, happened upon a moonless night. I impacted high upon the unmarked and frost-laden barrier with a blinding flash. As a result, the visionary plans that were scribbled on note papers fell out of my overstuffed shirt pockets. They were scattered by gusts from a confused wind and forever lost. Some closely veiled goals escaped and cartwheeled along the rocky ground. Others burned in the wreckage. The wall-scraping descent was rapid. It produced a trail of electric-blue sparks that were only visible to survivors of The Wall.

I lost consciousness before hitting the frost-heaved ground. Pain is non-existent when one is comatose.

I awoke and began crawling from the twisted and charred carcass on elbows and knees. The silence was deafening, but somehow I managed to firmly press the numb palms of my tired hands against my ringing ears.

I was overcome, not by acrid smoke, but by an uncanny feeling of perfect relief!

I have absolutely no desire, whatsoever, to return to my former life. Looking back it was a life measured and quantified by someone else through in-kind hours, rules, deadlines, and restrictive budgets. Requests for my time were endless. I could not say "no" back then.

Today, light years from the smoldering crash site, I tenaciously hold onto my life's trusty compass—my God-given intuition. I first used it to discover The Woods in 1973. It, or I, has been lost ever since.

It is still pointing to The Woods and I will never misplace it again.

I sent out a form letter stating that I no longer would be available for the things I used to freely do. I would keep Wildcat Woods and the NU Arbor Day going only until their mission was fulfilled in April and May of 1996 respectively.

I had run far enough, and fast enough, to overcome the gravitational pull of The Wall. I never did look back, but soon discovered that I had overstretched other bounds too. Others deduced that I could lead by example, but not by committee. Failure was something that others chose. I could not, nor would not, make others follow me. My brand of leading by example did not encourage others to take the ball and run with it. Friends and allies were understanding, but hints of treason would sometimes waft from stilted conversations.

It is the penalty paid for forging ahead and not waiting for others to catch-up. It is the antithesis of playing-it-safe!

Each day we walk a narrowing path between chimera and profound wisdom.

There would be no more science fair judging, tree commission, extension advisory, or SWCD committee work. The Acorns to Oak teacher workshops, and tours of The Woods, would end.

I would never return to that life.

I have no regrets concerning my altruistic contributions. I know I made a positive difference in Nature's world because my love of 26 years, Teresa, told me so.

Today, I continue to serve as a 4-H advisor with my wife for Union County's oldest 4-H Club—The Claibourne Up & Coming 4-H Club. I am the no-charge caretaker of the ancient oaks and fresh planted trees at the century-old Richwood Fairgrounds. I continue to tend the trees at the Richwood Lake Park on my own time.

But mostly I am thinking about my next trip to The Woods!

Nature's Allegory

The text of today's sermon is from the Gospel according to another John.

To me, our non-denominational God is spelled N-A-T-U-R-E, and irrefutable evidence is unveiled each spring when God is most visible and creative!

The events and miracles of The Ministry of Jesus are recalled from the omnipotent wisdom of The Bible and of prophecies fulfilled. God's eternal promise is commemorated as Christians attend the seasonally-crowded churches of their choice.

Dressed in their finest apparel, they fellowship with others to publicly proclaim the glory of The Resurrection. However, we seem to overlook the unpretentious solitude of woodlands, wetlands, streams, ponds, and meadows where another resurrection—an effectual rebirth—is taking place.

Perhaps it is more than coincidental that spring and Easter occur at the same time?
Potted Easter lilies, wrapped in gold foil, neatly flank either side of the polished pulpit. Three miles distant, indefatigable wildflowers are growing randomly in the leaf-littered woods. Here, wide-eyed honeybees, on maiden flights of mission, diligently tend to the fragrant woodland blossoms in dot-to-dot fashion. The detailed symmetry of the petals confirms that God is not dead… just taken for granted!
Throughout the crowded pews, the familiar scent of open hymnals is ever present. Outside, in Nature, the warm drafts of spring are subtle, though surreal, in presenting a potpourri of fresh earthy aromas.
In sum and substance, we know God's House, but little of where God lives!

On cue, the obedient choirs rise and sing time-honored hymns to the Glory of God. In The Woods, dwarfed beneath the immensity of a centuries'-old white oak, I comfortably sit and listen to other exaltations. Itinerant meadowlarks, wrens, and wood thrushes sing unrehearsed praises in the present tense. The tireless titmouse alights within the oaken zenith and intercedes with ringing calls of: "Peter… Peter… Peter!" Then quickly flits away to repeat it again and again!

Peter?

In church, I stir and notice the painstaking artistry of the stained glass. I wonder how many around me have ever observed a sun drenched Eastern bluebird through binoculars. Mystically the lenses brilliantly transform into an amplified kaleidoscope of iridescent blues, orange, and stainless white.

The former is of civilization, the latter is of God.

The congregation's stewardship is often measured by baroque collection plates, passed with starched protocol. In Nature, the planting of a tree, the cultivation of colorful flowers, and the erection of bird nesting boxes are truer forms of greater service.

I stir again and scrutinize the painted plaster ceilings, detailed architecture, and ornate light fixtures. In Nature I lift up my eyes to see an infinite cerulean sky. It is animated with the synchronous flight of blue-winged teal preparing to splash the seamless tea-colored surface of a restored wetland below.

Suddenly... resplendently... all things are revealed!

"The Sermon on The Mount," The Sea of Galilee, The River Jordan, The Garden, and The Wilderness were all out-of-doors in Nature! Those friendly admonishments: "Consider the lilies..." "Look at the sparrows..." "I am the vine..." and mustard seed faith all come back to me as Things of Nature!

This spring start anew!

Awaken to a fiery-orange sunrise, or contemplate of a rose-blushed sunset. Listen for the wake-up call of the crimson cardinal singing from the apex of a bud-swollen maple. Relax to the robin's twilight melodies as another spring day is lullabied to sleep. Perceive the twinkling stars of a moonless night, or traipse in the tranquility of the Full Moon's pastel light. It's the only color that can be felt upon one's skin.

Faithfully continue to attend and support the church of your choice and needs. Hear the enlightened theological interpretations of God's love for us.

Additionally, seek out a venue in Nature. Experience with all your senses, God's love for you, face-to-face, in the ecological renewal of life known as The Spring!

For this is God's encore Resurrection for the living!

Amen.

The Rockenbaugh Farm, 1996

Thirty-four years after dad and mom bought the farm, it has become a different farm.

It is no longer 100 acres of tired land, but rather 92 acres of renewed land. Gone are the undersized soybeans. The rare corn crop is no longer a roll of the dice. Wheat, a commodity that never grew attached to our farm, is out of the picture.

The oaks and hickories that defined my pre-teen wilderness are alive and well. In addition, we have planted over 20 acres of former crop land to young trees. Trees such as: red, pin, swamp white, white, and bur oak, sweetgum, walnut, sugar maple, Norway spruce, white and green ash. But mostly green ash and pin oak. Today a simple green and white Tree Farm sign claims its spot in the fencerow. Gone is the aged billboard and other roadside harlots.

The farm was eager to receive the gifts of restored wetlands. There are now two wetlands with two more being built. There is a pond where land once sat saturated beneath an impromptu willow. The cows, a slow pony, and 1200 white ducks are memories. Wild ducks, white tail deer, Eastern bluebirds, Canada Geese, monarch butterflies, and muskrat are now the farm's self-sustaining livestock.

The large cottonwood, in the former barnyard, has done well. It has fathered (and mothered) another generation; a generation that will not be plowed asunder by a red two-bottom plow.

Marysville has moved ever closer. Houses are built along its eastern fencerow and across the road to the north. An over illuminated bi-lingual golf driving range, complete with unplumb bi-lingual billboards, shove-up against the western fencerow. To the south, a highway runs through it. The monstrous power lines continue to hum, snap, and pop depending upon the weather. A red tail hawk regularly hunts from its erector set supports. Below the gangly power line tower is chest-high switchgrass. Gone are the dusty broadleaves associated with poverty farming.

The farm is enrolled in the Conservation Reserve Program and in The Wetland Reserve Program. The government, remember, will never be out of my debt for the crime committed in placing a special-interest highway through our land, or its eagerness to help out public utilities in condemning land for power lines and oil lines.

I can cooperate, as well as oppose, anything or anyone to death.

The 4 acre pond was established after exhaustive months of cooperation with the contractors' project estimators.

It was unrestrained cooperation that brought 13,000 new trees, 4 wetlands, and 8 acres of switchgrass to the farm. Of course, none of this "just happened." It took insistence and perseverance to site a 4 acre wetland after the site was earlier dismissed because of design constraints. The switchgrass seed was provided free of charge in exchange for allowing it to grow for at least 11 years. It, the trees, and the wetlands will grow forever as far as I am concerned.

The Months of Nature

January is The Winter. Everything else is late fall or early spring

It is a month that always features cold powdery snow. Sometime after January 12th there is a predictable few days, or hours, of warmer temperatures with heavy rain. Just as quickly, winter returns for good.

Some of the most beautiful sunny days, and starry nights, are found in January.

It is January's Full Moon that depicts this month in Nature best.

At this time of the year, when the Big Dipper is scraping the frozen northern horizon, the well-overhead Full Moon shines brightest through an atmosphere of high pressure fronts. Its light, even its color, can be felt upon one's skin!

Orion, the only hunter allowed on the farm, crosses the upper-southern sky in futile pursuit of the Seven (6) Sisters. The Full Moon lights his way. It does no good.

If by chance there is snow cover when the moon is full, the landscape reveals all of its nocturnal secrets. Owls can be seen gliding goldenrod-high, or poised alert in barren oak branches. A trotting fox does not go unnoticed across the ice of the frozen wetland. Rabbits join together to hop, skip, and jump across the old abandoned road—never straying far from familiar pinkish-colored trails. The Full Moon is their delight and enemy.

It is a time of "chick-a-dee-dee-dee!" and the persistent sharp chirps of flashing Cardinals playing wing tip tag in tangled borders of pasture rose and hawthorns. In the quiet woods one can hear a brown creeper spiraling-up a solemn bur oak. Is it the creeper's myopic concentration—hunger—that allows me to watch from arm's length, or is it simply the bird's trusting instinct? I do not know.

The Canada geese, local clans, continue to join-up en-masse and forage around the area. No longer are they a high altitude V-formation of migrants, but rather year-round residents. The cloud, or swarm, of Canadas are somewhat indecisive as to where to forage each day. Factions of 9, 13, or 26 drop out of the confusion and head for familiar corn stubble in a cursive, though low altitude, V-formation. By evening they rendezvous and settle down somewhere in Union County

Horned owls can be heard hooting, while screech owls winnow their wavering trills. Rarely, far off to the southwest of the farm, I hear the "Who cooks for you… who cooks for you… who cooks for you all?" questioning of a barred owl. January is for owls.

Snow cover benefits those hungry for ripened seeds atop summer's stalks now brown with purpose. The snow often enables mice and birds to walk the crust and reach protein-rich seed heads now bent under their own weight. Scattered in the snow are leftover crumbs and cross stitch tracks of fulfillment. Yet another "weed" offered ample reason to end the negative societal bias of these plants—native, or alien.

Between hickories and oaks, the snow reveals the telegraph line travels of a fox squirrel. The fleet-footed tracks of this beautiful, though hungry, resident offer an occasional in-line "dig." It is evidence of an exhumed treasure and further proof that there is no substitute for preparation. There is a time to play and a time to eat. For now, here is no dilly-dallying around. The snow is too great of a handicap in the stratagem of prey vs. predator.

It is in January, when snow is brushed from tannin-rich oak leaf litter, that the blanketed world of green is revealed. Teachings that life is absent in the "dead of winter" are contradicted. I find lush, though frost-laden, leaves of common blue violets, fivefingers cinquefoil, and teasel rosettes.

January is the ephemeral winter.

February's greatest contribution to 40 Degree North Latitude's civilization and beast is the cognizant recognition of increased daylight. For too many months the sun has stolen low across the south. February is the welcomed light at the end of the groundhog's, as well as, the winter's tunnel.

Abbreviated February is a month of incongruity. I sense it in inconsistent temperatures and snowfall. It is a month that hints of spring yet delivers winter cold and snow. Wildlife sense the resurrection photo-chemically. Their instincts confirm what I can only wish.

Book biologists and 12-guage conservationist tell me that February is too early for the increasing number of two hink-honking Canada geese that I watch. They emphatically state that pair bonding is still a month away. The Canada geese that I know, or profess to know, are breaking the rules. In fact I have witnessed pairs of Canada geese in December, January, and February, as well as in March! They slice the post twilight darkness of February with the same hink-honking landings as they do in the proper passionate months of March and April. In Nature there are no absolute rules, only patterns to draw conclusions from. I have witnessed isolated pairs of Canada geese acting-out the same territorial protectiveness in winter as well as spring.

I have heard a murder of crows caw-cawing in the moonless February night. I suspect an owl was the object of their wrath. I once held that even crows rested at night. Now I'm not certain that there are any limits to what crows do, or when they do it.

Those sunny and warm(er) mornings of late February entice Mr. Cardinal to practice, with incomplete verse, its sweet territorial love song. He is found glowing atop the tree's highest branch, as though to say: "I must be heard as well as seen!"

Brighter, longer, and warmer days will serve to perfect his song and purpose. Of course the tufted titmice are scurrying around The Woods, and other neighboring woodlots, with their impatient and incessant whistles of "Peter… Peter… Peter!" This will last through March, or until silenced by the pressing responsibilities of fatherhood.

By February 27th I have seen and heard northbound killdeers. The robins and turkey vultures are seen by those with vision beyond windshields and calendars. They are delivered here by the same erratic warm drafts that blow fresh litter into, and hibernating litter out of, leaning fencerows. Scouting Eastern meadowlarks, calling from frosty barbwire, flinch and glance at the stirrings below. With a second look they dismiss this phenomenon as non-threatening, albeit unnatural.

March has two distinct personalities that have no relationships, or connectedness.

It is a season of landscape dreariness, as well as beauty. It is a month of snow squalls one day and shirt sleeves the next. March can be as dismal as life ever gets. One can stand in ankle-deep mud and seemingly hear water seeping through worm tunnels. Even the cold gray mist of ugly March days seems audible as it rolls into pin oak, or last year's clumps of orchardgrass. These days fail to produce any wildlife activity. Even the raucous call of a blue jay, or a stirring in the switchgrass, would be welcome and reason enough to continue living.

However, these days in March are outnumbered by increased intimations of spring. Some Eastern bluebirds stay and outlast the winter. But only in March do I began to hear the soft warblings that are the signature of the blue jewels. Chipmunks venture out of subterranean shelters found on either side of the old abandoned road cross tile. Food, while a primary concern, takes second place to running in and out of cover.

Lt. Colonels of the red-winged blackbirds, announce plans to invade the grasslands and wetlands upon the farm. Their verbal checks and tee-err notes, along with gurglings of konk-la-ree and o-ka-lay, announce intentions of a seasonal encampment. They will make sure the grasslands and wetlands never fall asleep during the summer. Woe to any sojourner unprepared for the clamor associated with trespassing into their territories. From their harrier-like advantage, they bombard with relentless verbal abuse. One is relieved to finally escape from the noise and unintentional infractions of red-winged rules.

On March 18th I walk to the hazelnut patch along the east side of the old abandoned road. There I will find, without fail, the hazel's tiny scarlet flower that is indifferent to more patient prognosticators of spring.

The first maniacal laughs of the yellow-shafted flickers are heard. Their jungle-like calls will continue until fall. When not hollering, the flicker is an accomplished drummer beyond compare.

The aerobatic tree swallows return just as they left, dropped-off by some southern zephyr. I often wonder if they ever tire of flying.

Formerly in-over-their-heads in mud, the spring peepers emerge to "peep" and drown out all other terrestrial sounds. Even after leaving their performance, I continue to hear the echoes of their chorus of peeps in my head.

The wetlands are now awake.

Traffic is busy on the surface as northern shovellers, ringnecks, woodies, hoodies, and mallards compete for food that I cannot see. On the pond, lesser scaups and coots enliven the waterscape. The fatigued scaups seem content to ride the ripples like a bobber for a week or two. The American Coot is always moving. Nicknamed: pond chicken, this character struts in the water like a chicken does on land.

The blue heron fishes from the shallows of both pond and wetland. They only leave when the open water freezes-over, but are always back in March.

Upland, I hear rufous-sided towhees thrashing in the woodland border's leaf litter.

At twilight I watch the American woodcock do his vertical air show, complete with sound, for some shy hen. Year after year they return to the same grassy waterway for an encore performance.

By late March the buzzards are soaring above the farm. For now the warming woodlands and fields are generating thermals.

The month of March is the open front door of life on Earth. All that are worthy may now follow and enter.

Get in line, it is about to get busy!

All that one needs to do is step outside in April to smell the glorious spring!

Some of My Favorite Journal Entries from John

–Teresa

February 25, 1984

What a rate child of the winter it is, that does not anticipate the resurrection of life, the <u>Hope</u> eternally known as the SPRING! By the Grace of God.

March 10, 1984

Just experienced my 1st flying squirrel. Alive and well… In the Woods Nature Reserve, God through nature always amazes me, Always. What I saw today will not be forgotten. It cost no admission and was not staged. Yet no movie or book could portray the Beauty in motion that I witnessed. This event further supports my belief: 1) God has a deliberate purpose for each of his earthly creations 2) That it is the simple and subtle, everyday events in nature that constitutes real life and real living 3) That <u>God</u> has no match in his majestic plans. We search each day for sophistication and complexity… Futile to its daily end. The flying Squirrel is a miracle to behold.

I can only remember 4 times in my life at Being So HAPPY AND EXCITED…
Meeting my wife
Seeing each of our three sons born
And now the Eastern Bluebird in the area of Box #7… NEAT!

Noticed numerous Eastern Towhees, never before been here, for habitat was not conducive to them. Now they are numerous, along with son sparrows. Already there is life among the TSI (Timber Stand Improvement) Cuttings. This is yet another example of how we have "manipulated" wildlife habitat. ODOT said, "We had not attempted it in the DEIS (Draft Environmental Impact Statement). Red-winged Blackbirds sat perched on a single stem of grass without collapsing to the ground. I shall never figure it out!

I am at my very best in NATURE. I am at my worst in SOCIETY. It is Society that corrupts one's spirit. In The Woods I am with God, in Society He is with me even at my worst. I acknowledge God and Praise Him in (Nature) at the Woods. Often in Society I am not the Person he wants me to be and I am ashamed.

I go to The Woods and find myself praising creation (NATURE)—NO WHERE ELSE DO I DO THAT...NO WHERE ELSE DO I FEEL COMFORTABLE WITH GOD AND MYSELF.\ God has blessed me with a Wonderful Family and with them in the Woods it is a Perfect Family. Nature, Not church is how I learn of God's Love for me.

I shall use the wonders of Nature to call attention to God's amazing works and use of seasons to show they story of the Resurrection!

In Nature all is right.
Nature is not two-faced.
Nature does not gossip.
There is divine purity in simple nature... unspoiled, innocent and peace.

I was asked, recently, by a youngster (who was playing a word game) who was my best friend... Thinking as I thought a child would think I could not answer. I realized that I had no "Buddy Friend" and answered "myself." I was my best Friend. I have had friends—Best Friends in my youth. I grew away from these friendships as I learned the insincerity and futility of relationships. I enjoy my time and solitude.

Reflecting on the Question again... I would have answered... "My wife, Teresa." Truly God has presented me with a friend for life and forever with Teresa. Everything that is right is Teresa. If I had Teresa, my sons, and the "Woods" all together I would have it made!

December 2, 1984

I am called to Nature in subdued desperation. <u>No One</u> is assured of the length of one's earthly life and indeed Nature will outlive us all. In Nature, one is made aware of how insignificant we are in her presence. Like eternity, she will continue on. If we are Christians that we are to be, our gift of eternal life will be the comparison of Nature's Renewal.

I must get on with my work in the Woods...Now!

September 2, 1985

Nature, like myself, does not recognize Special Interests, Politics, Greed and the Self-Inflated EGOS. What price can be paid to reimburse the value of the silence that grows so well in the Woods? (Silence, in Nature is a non-renewable resource. Once lost... It is gone forever. The Woods is a source of Wonder even for my 4 month old daughter...She stares with a big smile at the Waving leaves from her vista below.

November 3, 1985

The Woods is a Cathedral without the Frill. It is God's special Sanctuary... A chapel. Not unlike man's relationships with God-Jesus. The Woods is a Spiritual Gift preserved for those who are perceptive to the Beautiful Gifts of God.

<u>THERE IS NOT WILDERNESS IN UNION COUNTY TODAY!!</u>

December 27, 1985
10:10 pm – 11:30 pm
    Went to the Woods with Brodie to walk. It was one of those perfect nights…
    Full Moon Bright
    Clear High Pressure
    Snow Covered
    We walked searching for 3-wheelers that had violated the trails and non-trails.

January 1, 1986
    Went to the Woods/Farm to work, discovered Rocks and Moses with Cale… FUN!!
    I am learning the scents of wood very well.
    Hickory, at times, smells of Black pepper
    Ash smells unique, I guess
    Oak like no other smells sweet, strong like a logger's camp…
    Teresa brought Brodie, Caleb, T.J. and Tracie down along with delicious Hot Potato Soup. I love Teresa so much! The Boys stayed.

March 15, 1986
    Ron helped place tops on Cottontail Hilton of his design, the brush pile not finished. Flu-bug sapped my strength after Ron left for home to California. Ron will be missed until his return… Soon, I hope. I need his help. He is a good Brother and Friend.

April 20, 1986
    The absence of entries after 3/14/86 in no way reflects the absence of hard work.
    God, in his majestic plan, has arranged weather in such a way that we have been able to work every weekend. Thank you, God! Charlie Watkins came with Jim Bartlett to cut old Swamp White Oak for saw logs. 5 trees total all over 115 years of age a 30"dbh most certainly the oldest over
    150 years.
    Cost: $25.00 to cut down
              $15.00 to buck saw logs
              $40.00 Total

May 30, 1986
    Caleb's Own
                BIRDS
    Flying high, high, high in the sky
    Red, Blue, Yellow, Brown flying all over town
    Up, down all around
    Making all kinds of chirping sounds
    In the shrubs one, two, three
    I saw one way up in a tree.

November 11, 1986

It is important that I write a Land Ethic for now & forever.

My Land Ethic for the rest of the world....

Ethic:

Any single element in a system of ethics

Ethical, character, custom, essential Quality, own character, one's own of or conforming to moral standards, conforming to the standards of conduct of a given profession or ground the system or code of morals

Moral:

Manners, customs relating to dealing with or capable of making the distinction between Right and Wrong in conduct.

Principles, standards or habits with respect to right or wrong in conduct ethics and civilized standards of right or wrong based on the principles of Right conduct rather than on law or customs

DUTY and JUDGEMENT

AS of this writing there is no wilderness in the clay soils area of Western Paris Township or even in Union County, Ohio

I am, at best, but a sojourner on this planet, Earth. Land is soil and land is dirt. My land ethic describes land as a living medium for plant life, soil is alive and precious–the place where wildflowers erupt and trees begin their upward ascent.

Land is soil – Good Earth Soil is forever, I hope. Soil is life!

WE must be in a grand hurry to be patient. We must start today.

Conservation without an inclination to preservation cannot succeed. To be a Preservationist is not to be (stagnant) but to be active.

To save the things of Nature should have started yesterday.

My land ethic involves the following:

Trees of forests

Wildflowers

Wildlife

Birds

Soils

Grasses

Water

December 22, 1986

Nature and environmental protection must increase while I decrease. Not unlike the Christian's ethic of so long ago.

December 24, 1986

12:10 AM

To persist in the face of adversity is the perennial miracle of Nature. JRR

Life's greatest revelation is the peaceful co-existence found in the things of Nature. JR

Nature teaches us to persist over every adversity with the promise of renewal.

February 1987

Let us begin today to preserve and protect the things of nature by picking up our trail and tracks laid down yesterday in mere thought.

Let us progress, not by proxy but by individual efforts to that ethic which benefits…those remaining things of Nature… Still WILD, FREE and INNOCENT.

Let us invest in generations to come. Preservation, not just conservation, in time they will find gratitude with our forethought and not bitterness with our environmental negligence.

It is the effort that begins in the heart and spreads to the soul. Once discovered it is all-consuming. It guides us to leave footprints upon the Woodland floor and nothing more.

After all, we are but sojourners upon the planet, Earth charged with spreading love and stewardship for his mighty works.

In the Nature we happen upon, we learn of God's love for man.

By the Nature we leave, we learn of Man's love for God and all the generations to follow.

February 3, 1988

The Bible is full of many stories, miracles and teachings. Why do relinquish ourselves to live by their experience and accept their history? God is still around performing miracles for "NO-SHOW" audiences. God, I want to experience your presence HEAD-ON and person to person. I am sorry mankind has put you on the shelf. I haven't!! AMEN!

September 1, 1988

NOTE: Wooded acreage in Union County today 277,800 acreage 18,000 Wooded Min.

Woodlands 13,060 Specified Woodlands 18,000 acres Max Woodlands 23,940 acres

1991 Conservation (Government – State)

Money Rules – Money Regulations – Talk Money

There is NO ONE – NOT ONE that thinks like me. I am alone in my conservation ETHIC that Promotes LIFE – ALL LIFE! Me and Nature!

In the loneliness of my convictions is the truth that ecology is sustained by preserving life. BENEFIT!!

Wetlands, no matter their size or location are an oasis of life.

In a Wetland, I have seen Mallards, Blue-winged Teal, American Coot, Egret, Heron, American Bittern, Canada Goose, Muskrat, Deer, Tree Swallow, Frogs and Dragonflies.

The Cabin, December 25, 1991

And so it began…

Earlier in this journal, Jan. 1986, the idea of a cabin began. The 60–70 year old Swamp White Oaks standing, then falling to become 14' 6" long logs for a cabin in "the Woods."

February 1991 I continued to work on Brodie's car in the Cold Barn.

March 1991 Still working on car can hear meadowlarks on fence outside.

September 1991 Finished Cabin floor

October 1991 Worked in Cabin

November 1991 Thanksgiving in Cabin

December 19 91 Worked in Cabin… Many beautiful sunsets this month.

Eastern Bluebird seen 12/23/91

The Presbyterian Church is building a new addition… MONEY! MONEY! MONEY!

I believe in God and Jesus and in synoptic gospels of Mathew, Mark, Luke and John. I believe in life and Nature. I believe the Loving God is loving nature. I believe that God created everything BUT in long, complex, magnificent perfection. Furthermore, to reduce baggage I would keep John 13:34 and "Be Happy"! "And I am giving a new commandment to you now—love each other just as I have loved you." John 13:34

God and his wonderful works are alive in Nature every second of every day of every year. Jesus is the ticket to continue on. Forgiveness and love are the two greatest gifts known to but now known by man. FORGIVE! FORGIVE! FORGIVE! In Nature (GOD) there is peace there is harmony there is a purpose. God is Love! Nature is God revealed! Nature is Now!

I plan to plant more trees in 1992 and to manage more wetlands. I plan on getting back to the purposeful simplicity of learning and doing at the Woods!

Teresa bought a very old "Warm Morning" stove for me as a perfect 20th wedding anniversary gift. Its life to date had been spent in Union County. It would go in the cabin and remain loyal to friends and visitors of this Union County oak log cabin. The following weekend I found a gray screech owl roosting comfortably in the cabin. It found its way out through the east window opening.

It would soon be time to consider building a door to fit the sturdy frame and to install the two imperfect windows that were donated to us. The west-facing door began as a piece of 1/2" plywood neatly filling the door opening. On either side of the plywood, 3/4" planed random width swamp white oak boards, homegrown, were secured. The door, now two inches thick was secured directly to the logs with heavy-type hinges.

The windows were installed and trimmed with rough-cut swamp white oak boards

A simple loft was constructed in the east half of the cabin.

There were plenty of floor joists that joined two large oak logs that crisscrossed in the center of the 12' x 12' cabin floor area. Their intersection was placed upon the centermost boulder of nine. Exterior plywood was nailed directly to the joists to form the subfloor. Random width rough-cut swamp white oak boards were nailed directly through the subfloor and into the joists. The sawmill's blade left excellent radial marks in the boards. The oak floor had character and needed nothing else.

The best thing that happened in 1991 was the finishing of the Log Cabin. Thanks to Teresa – Not Me—the cabin became a real place, a living place. The Floor was installed in late August/early Sept. The "Warm Morning" coal/wood stove, a 20th anniversary gift from Teresa made a place with a personality and purpose.

Opening the doors the cabin smells of unique sweetness of Oak.

We celebrated "Thanksgiving" in the cabin. Teresa cooked the traditional Thanksgiving meal (Turkey, Mash. Pot, Gravy, rolls, Cranberry (jellied) in a can, Dressing, scalloped corn and Fresh-perked coffee on the stove and ice tea.

It was a Good Thanksgiving.

The Cabin that was constructed has served our families Thanksgivings for over 15 years.

About the Author

–written by John's son, Brodie Rockenbaugh

John R. Rockenbaugh died peacefully on Friday morning, November 18th at his home in Richwood, Ohio following a brief battle with cancer.

A 1970 graduate of Marysville High School, John was employed at Bob Chapman Ford in Marysville from 1971 to 1997 specializing in new vehicle pre-delivery. In 1975, he was the winner of Ford Motor Company's, Great Lakes Region Job-Skilled competition. He served as an elected Supervisor for the Union Soil and Water Conservation District from 1989 to 1992. John was selected as one of twelve Ohio Division of Wildlife/SWCD Wildlife Specialists in 1998, where he passionately served until his passing. He is a life member of the Marysville FFA Alumni Association and a member of the Ohio Tree Farm Committee. John served on the Ohio State University Farm Science Review-Gwynne Conservation Area committee and the Glacier Ridge Metro Park Advisory Group. John loved to read and write. He served as a column writer and Editorial Board member for "The Ohio Woodland Journal."

Following a noon day thunderstorm in July of 1973, John's true passion and inspiration for learning and sharing land ethics and ecology was realized…The Woods Nature Reserve was conceived. The Woods became a sanctuary for John and his ever-growing family to visit, practice conservation and share in the seasonal wonders. In 1985, The Woods became Ohio Tree Farm #2174, certified for Timber Stand Improvement efforts. In 1991, John and his family completed a humble 14' by 14' cabin from swamp white oak logs where family Thanksgivings have taken place since. John's pastimes at The Woods included creating, restoring and enjoying wetlands, vernal pools, grasslands, woodlands, a 4-acre pond, shelter house and foot trails with his family.

"A thing is right when it tends to preserve the integrity, stability, and beauty of the biotic community. It is wrong when it tends otherwise." (A Sand County Almanac by Aldo Leopold)

John passionately shared his love for what Aldo Leopold described as "good country" by instructing and encouraging conservation, land ethics and the study of all things in nature for present and future generations. His love for wildlife and enduring habitats, conservation practices, wildlife interests, and wildlife concerns helped him serve the residents and landowners of Union County. Thousands of students, throughout Ohio, now have a greater appreciation for the land and its resources as a result of In-Pool Wetland and Freshwater studies, Arbor Day events, Master Gardeners for Backyard Wildlife programs and countless hours of educational programming John conducted.

In the words of many, after his passing, "John has left the world better than he found it."

Epilogue

This is a story of my best friend of 40 years and of an inspiration that came to John from God during a walk in "The Woods." As John walked through the woods that day in 1973, he said to me, "Teresa, God said, "Do something with my nature" —So it became "The Woods" Nature Reserve.

For many years after this book was written, my husband, John Rockenbaugh, continued his love for wildlife and God's creations. His many journals were written every time he visited The Woods. He continued walking The Woods and learning and teaching. My favorite journal entries include the many varieties of birds John witnessed in his walks: Mocking Bird, Red-Winged Blackbird, Tufted Titmouse (He loved to mock his sound "Peter! Peter! Peter!"), Chicadees, Great Blue Herron, Canadian Geese, Mallards and two of his favorites—Bluebird and Red-Tailed Hawk. John loved to describe the deer as they browsed the plants. His identification of wildflowers and plant life was far more knowledgeable than any College graduate.

His legacy continues through our children, grandchildren, family, friends, and all those who crossed paths.

"It is a surprising and memorable, as well as valuable experience, to be lost in the woods any time."
— Henry David Thoreau, *Walden*

"Heaven is under our feet as well as over our heads."
— Henry David Thoreau, *Walden*

On Saturday 1-10-98 John wrote:

"Full Moon tonight.

I hear the female mallard quack-quacking on the Big Wetland in the dark, rather the pastel light of the Full Moon.

It is almost twenty-five years since God inspired me to create The Woods on that Hot July afternoon in 1973.

So much has changed here. I will sit upon the large square rock on the east side of the cabin and bathe in the ethereal moonlight that floods the logs and rich mortar chinking.

On Earth, this is the most beautiful spot I know and feel. I can feel the beauty of this moon-splashed location.

Four candles light the interior of the cabin, but God's Moon lights the outside walls.

It is fitting, I guess to share with my journal the Anticipation-Anxiety I have for the coming week."

This is John's very last journal entry:

On Tuesday, January 13, 1998, at 11:00 AM, I will interview for a job as a Wildlife Specialist for the Union Soil and Water Conservation District.

Yes, I am qualified- I just know. I want this important job so much. It will represent the change I want and the fulfillment I need. I had total support of my beautiful family. If there was one reason I would not try for the job, it would be the fact that my family may suffer financially. Each in their own way removed that concern from my heart. I am free to pursue my dream. I know that God knows my anxiousness and my desire."

A week later John became the Union County Wildlife Specialist and within a year was back to his financial security for the family. And with his personality and love to teach everyone he met about God's creation, he left a legacy for Union County that will live on for many years.

I wish all reading this book could have met my best friend and husband, John Rockenbaugh!!

Dreams coming full circle.

John being able to fulfill his passion of

the Love of Nature

"I learned this, at least, by my experiment: that if one advances confidently in the direction of his dreams, and endeavors to live the life which he has imagined, he will meet with a success unexpected in common hours."
— Henry David Thoreau, *Walden: Or, Life in the Woods*

04/28/2011

John,
Thank you for sharing your knowledge of and enthusiasm for nature. You have touched many young people. You are an inspiration!
Sincerely,

Thank you for all you do for our schools and students! Words can't express our gratitude and the impact you have!

John, You are a huge inspiration to all ages of learners.
Laurie
Creekview teacher
passion!

you need you
You are a gift
Please fight
You're an inspiration

John – You are a very special person to me and to everyone in Manville School. Your visits have meant the world to me and all arts. Your knowledge and smile on our faces to seeing you. You used to bring caterpillars with my daughters. You've helped my interests and always give

We all love it when you come. Your hair with the tassel. Look forward to it each year! A teacher told me you gave her a tiny pine years ago its so tall now! You are loved + needed Eighty!
Your fascinating info!
You are so giving
We love you!

John –
Thanks for your continued dedication + passion! You are a true steward of the land! Happy New Year! Thanks for being a part of our program!
Janine

128

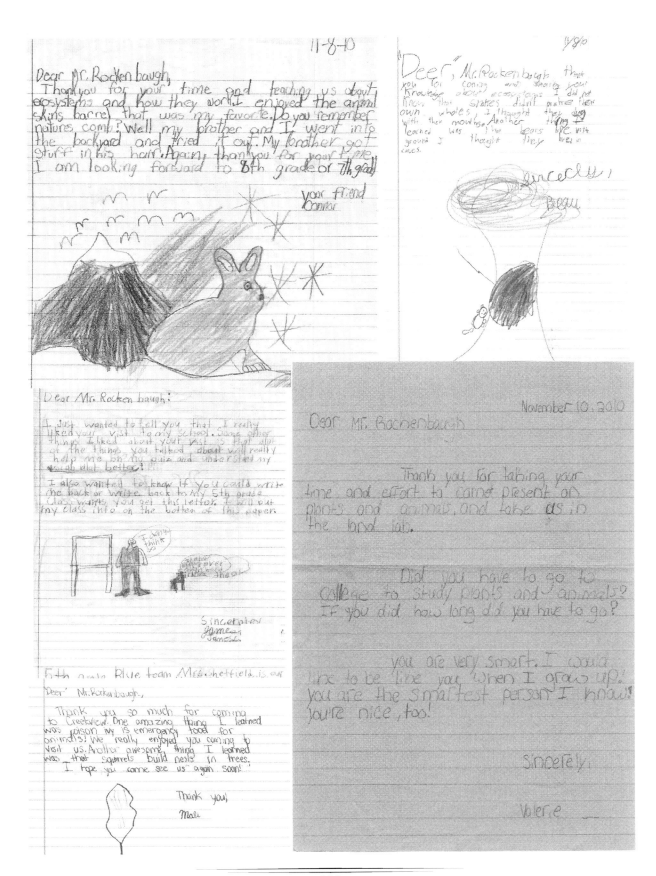

11-8-10

Dear Mr. Rockenbaugh,
Thank you for your time and teaching us about ecosystems and how they work. I enjoyed the animal skins barrel, that was my favorite. Do you remember natures comb? Well my brother and I went into the backyard and tried it out. My brother got stuff in his hair. Again, thank you for your time. I am looking forward to 8th grade or 7th grade!

your friend
Connor

11/8/10

"Deer" Mr. Rockenbaugh, thank you for coming and sharing your knowledge about ecosystems. I did not know that snakes didn't make their own wholes, I thought they dug with their mouths. Another thing I learned was that bears live with ground I thought they live in caves.

Sincerely,
Beau

Dear Mr. Rockenbaugh:

I just wanted to tell you that I really liked your visit to my school. Some other things I liked about your visit is that alot of the things you talked about will really help me on my quiz and understand my vocab alot better!

I also wanted to know if you could write me back or write back to my 5th grade class whats you get this letter. I will put my class info on the bottom of this paper.

I don't think so.

Sincerely,
James Janosik

5th grade Blue team Mrs. hetfield is our

November 10, 2010

Dear Mr. Rockenbaugh

Thank you for taking your time and effort to come present on plants and animals, and take us in the land lab.

Did you have to go to college to study plants and animals? If you did how long did you have to go?

You are very smart. I would like to be like you when I grow up! You are the smartest person I know! You're nice, too!

Sincerely,

Valerie

Dear Mr. Rockenbaugh,

Thank you so much for coming to Creekview. One amazing thing I learned was poison ivy is emergancy food for animals! We really enjoyed you coming to visit us. Another awesome thing I learned was that squirrels build nests in trees. I hope you come see us again soon!

Thank you,
Mali

Terri,

... something I've been wanting to do ... personally ... for quite some time. I still miss John's wit & wisdom today! Our paths didn't cross often enough, but when they did, it was a quality, memorable time spent. I'm sure John never realized what a positive influence he was on all of us WS's, though he would have humbly down played anyhow. That was just the kind of guy he was. Whatever he could do to help you out, he gladly accomodate. John had quite a few of those "Rock-isms", like "fix it or shac it" or "healthy cultures don't bite." We still like to share those with folks today.

I recently came across this quote I feel really fit John's life and example he left us to model: "Work for a cause, not for applause, Live life to express not to impress. Don't strive to make your presence noticed, just make your absence felt..."

The "seeds" that John planted are still growing today. And the seed bank he left to Union SWCD is still being sown into young lives today, to ensure the best possible care of natural resources will always be there to take care of us!

Your friend & co-worker in conservation,

Tim

Acknowledgments

As my past becomes my present, this book is bringing to everyone a magnificent trip through our family's fight for, and love of, nature. This book was lived, dreamed, and followed through my last four years after the loss of my best friend.

Many aspects of John's story were shared and influenced by my son-in-law, Justin Wills, my daughters-in-law, Tami Rockenbaugh and Abby Rockenbaugh, and John's father, Dorance "Rocky" Rockenbaugh, who inspired John, myself, our two oldest boys (Brodie and Caleb) to live life to its fullest, love unconditionally, and be gentle and kind to everyone you meet.

Other influential people include John Hixson, Luke Miller, Mike Heisey, Chrissy Hoff, and many other staff at Glacier Ridge Metro Park, Perry Orndorff, Matt Staley, Terri Gravett, Bill Lynch, Bobby Chapman, Jim Bartlett, Suzi Clarridge, Donna Daniel, Tim Daniel, and countless teachers and students at Creekview, Bunsold and Navin Schools in Marysville, Ohio.

All of these, and many more, made John's love of nature and wildlife more rewarding, and I thank each and every one.

T-Shirt Memory Quilt created by John's mother.

"Books are the treasured wealth of the world and the fit inheritance of generations and nations."
— Henry David Thoreau, *Walden*

"The smallest seed of faith is better than the largest fruit of happiness."
—Henry David Thoreau, *Walden*

"Every child begins the world again, to some extent, and loves to stay outdoors, even in wet and cold. It plays house, as well as horse, having an instinct for it...At last we know not what it is to live in the open air, and our lives are domestic in more senses than we think."
— Henry David Thoreau, *Walden*

"Let us spend one day as deliberately as Nature."
— Henry David Thoreau, *Walden*

"Children, who play life, discern its true law and relations more clearly than men, who fail to live it worthily, but who think that they are wiser by experience, that is, by failure."
— Henry David Thoreau, *Walden*

Quotes from Thoreau Source: Thoreau, Henry D. (1854), Walden.

Made in the USA
Middletown, DE
10 March 2023